Baby or Bust

One Woman's Journey through Unsuccessful
IVF and How to Make Peace with It

LOUISE KEARINS

First published by Ultimate World Publishing 2025
Copyright © 2025 Louise Kearins

ISBN

Paperback: 978-1-923425-05-7
Ebook: 978-1-923425-06-4

Louise Kearins has asserted her rights under the Copyright, Designs and Patents Act 1988 to be identified as the author of this work. The information in this book is based on the author's experiences and opinions. The publisher specifically disclaims responsibility for any adverse consequences which may result from use of the information contained herein. Permission to use information has been sought by the author. Any breaches will be rectified in further editions of the book.

All rights reserved. No part of this publication may be reproduced, stored in or introduced into a retrieval system, or transmitted in any form, or by any means (electronic, mechanical, photocopying, recording or otherwise) without the prior written permission of the author. Any person who does any unauthorised act in relation to this publication may be liable to criminal prosecution and civil claims for damages. Enquiries should be made through the publisher.

Cover design: Ultimate World Publishing
Layout and typesetting: Ultimate World Publishing
Editor: Victoria Pickens

Ultimate World Publishing
Diamond Creek,
Victoria Australia 3089
www.writeabook.com.au

Testimonials

Baby or Bust is a deeply moving story that captures one of my closest friend's unfiltered reality of her journey of IVF, offering us all the opportunity to have a glimpse into her deepest hopes and heartbreaks. It was so admiring to read her honesty, not only about her own journey, but navigating the impact of infertility on her husband and their relationship.

The book is a testament to her resilience and faith in God as she shares the excruciating near-misses: getting pregnant only to lose each baby, and the emotional toll this cycle of hope and loss takes. I loved the way she balances her own narrative with her husband's perspective, which makes it relatable to couples.

What made this book powerful for me was my friend's willingness to be vulnerable. She doesn't sugarcoat the pain, but remains hopeful throughout her journey.

Leanne Heald

Baby or Bust is a brave and poignant account of Louise's experiences through trying to conceive, assisted pregnancy and pregnancy loss/miscarriage. I was moved by her honesty and lessons in learning to live again through active faith, intentional creativity and travel with purpose.

Caroline Pressey

To my beautiful sister. What a read! I thought I knew what you were going through, but I really had no idea! I'm so sorry you went through this without the desired outcome but so glad you are sharing your experience in Baby or Bust. You are an amazing human being, I am in absolute awe of your strength and determination and resilience.

Samantha Pledger

Disclaimer

While it's obvious that I am not in any way a medical person I want to be very clear that the processes I undertook during IVF may be different today as technology changes and procedures are refined and improved. The information I have included in relation to the IVF process is intended to be about my experience only.

Dedication

To my mum and sisters who have been with me throughout this journey and beyond—we are the dancing queens and super troupers.

To Dad, who still makes me laugh, thank you.

To my mum-in-law, whose rendition of *I will survive* I will never forget, and my sister-in-law, thank you.

To my husband David
It was a rocky road, but we made it through with God's help. We truly are islands in the stream, but hey, you say it best when you say nothing at all. Lue

Contents

Testimonials	iii
Disclaimer	v
Dedication	vii
Foreword	1
Chapter 1: Waiting	3
Chapter 2: The Dreaded Clock	7
Chapter 3: Doing it Naturally	19
Chapter 4: The Harvest	27
Chapter 5: Positively Pregnant	37
Chapter 6: The Angry Ant	51
Chapter 7: Deeds of the Desperate	59
Chapter 8: The Last Hoorah	67
Chapter 9: Return to Life	79
Afterword	95
Resources and Support Networks	101
About the Author	103
Speaker Bio	105

Foreword

When Louise first mentioned she wanted to write this book, I was surprised. From my perspective, the experience had such lasting consequences that I wanted to put them behind me. I simply didn't want to be reminded of that time in our lives.

As a man, I found the IVF process unkind. It felt as though the entire experience was designed around supporting your partner while leaving little room to process your own feelings and emotions. For us to come out the other side with nothing to show but scars—it was a deeply painful reality.

But as I watched Louise go about writing the book, as we listened to each other while discussing aspects of the book, as we talked about our experiences, as we laughed and recalled some of the funny things that happened along the way, and as we mourned the loss of what could have been, I realised that the experience tested and strengthened us both in ways that I didn't realise before.

Louise, who had already experienced more than most people before we started IVF, knows how to stand up and take courage; she has been doing it all her life. Louise sharing her story with such honesty is a testament to her strength and her desire to help others facing similar challenges.

Baby or Bust

This book is more than a memoir; it's a source of hope for anyone navigating the uncertainty of infertility. Louise's words remind us that even in the hardest moments, there is a way forward and that love and faith can carry us through the darkest days.

Whether you're facing your own fertility journey or simply seeking to understand and support someone who is, this book will move and inspire you. It's a story of courage, faith, and standing strong in the face of life's uncertainties.

For the men who may be reading this book, particularly if you are also facing your own fertility journey, I hope this book inspires and encourages you. Remember, you are loved, you are valuable, and you are worthwhile. Take care of yourself.

To my wife, you are a constant source of inspiration and encouragement. I couldn't be prouder of you for writing this book, and I'm honoured to share this journey with you. I hope your words touch others' hearts as deeply as mine.

Finally, to our Heavenly Father, who helps us both stand strong and picks us up when we fall...may you be glorified in all we do.

David Kearins

Chapter 1

Waiting

And so, after the rush, we sit. And we wait. Who are we? What are we doing here? And why are we here so avidly avoiding each other's eyes as if to say, I am not really here for the same reason you are? Am I? Could I be?

And yet we are all here, eyes glued to the television screen, listening, or at least pretending to listen to the banal conversation of morning TV, waiting for our name to be called. We shall be called, that's a given. Whether we are chosen, well that remains to be seen.

Baby or Bust

That was me. Waiting for the blood test. The blood test to determine how many times I would be having sex and when. 'Oh, surely it's not like that,' some would say. Or, 'You can't talk like that. It's a bit direct.' *You think?*

Sitting in the waiting room of the fertility clinic with other women, we were all there for the same reason. It didn't matter if you were young, older, pretty, fit, fat or even not so pretty. We all avoided each other's eyes as we sat, waiting for our name to be called. No one said a word or barely acknowledged each other. *Why?* I wanted to scream. We are all here for the same reason. We can't get pregnant. Why can't I ask you how you are going with it? Why can't we share our experience? Why can't we support each other? Do you know why? Let me tell you.

We can't talk because you are my competition. Statistically, In Vitro Fertilisation works for a small percentage of the population. You may not get there, but I am making damn sure I am doing everything to win that prize. *Move over ladies; I am having a baby!*

As I sit there I wonder what they are thinking. Surmising, for example. Oh no, surely I have a better chance than her because I am normal. Should she be here at all with that condition? You gotta be kidding, I am not like her. I must be a better candidate. Oh, it's my turn. I have been summoned, and off I skip, hopeful—ever hopeful.

You definitely are a pariah in the world of pregnant women if you decide to share your hopes and fears when you are in the IVF groove. You are a reminder to them that pregnancy doesn't always go the way you plan. You get dismissed and avoided as if being around you puts them at risk. I get it; if you are pregnant you want to protect your baby, but understand that I am not a threat. It doesn't matter because you are a reminder to them and they don't want to know. It's like when people put their fingers in their ears and sing *lalalalalala* so they can't hear what you're saying.

Waiting

It's them denying that what is happening to you will ever happen to them so they cannot even consider it. I don't blame them at all for that, I totally get it.

I have been talking with friends who are pregnant, and I have stopped myself talking about or even mentioning when I was pregnant. I can't share that with them because I have no kids of my own. It would be like me saying, "Yeah, you're pregnant now, but don't get your hopes up too much." That's my experience and I really don't want that to be their experience. I don't want to hurt them when they're in this vulnerable state so I just say nothing and listen to them as they express their feelings and hopes as they progress through each trimester. Mind you, it's taken me a long time to come to a place where I can converse with mums to be without running from the room and seeking alcohol—vodka, gin, whatever I can get my hands on.

Okay so if this is helpful to some people, then that is a success to me. This will be about what happened to me and how it affected me and my life then and now, which is thirteen years later. I don't want this to be a conventional type of book. I want you to learn from my experience. If you're a partner/friend/family member who wants to understand what's going on with whoever is going through fertility treatment, let this help you. If you're going through it yourself or have been there, maybe this will help you to express how you feel. Write notes in the margins, use it to share with others or just ponder things like, 'What the heck did she mean when she said…' or, 'Really, that's a load of BS!' or even, 'Wow someone actually feels the same as me, can this be?'

Baby or Bust

Where did I go?

Where did I go? Where did I go?

Somehow in the midst of it all

I lost the me that used to be

The me that used to sing uncaring

The me who'd dance around so daring

I don't know where she went

But I'd like to see her come back

She can never return, of that I'm sure

Just as clear as the dream's gone out the door

It doesn't mean that she's gone forever

She'll not be the same now, not ever

Is it because she's grown up and is older

Does the longer you live mean it's harder

Can she dance and sing without the tears

Falling down her cheeks untended

Can she look at the man she loves

And accept (with joy) that one plus one

doesn't always make three

Chapter 2

The Dreaded Clock

I want you to understand that our IVF journey started many years before we decided to do IVF. It was never an option I wanted to pursue and to be honest, I thought as my whole family were so fertile, I would never have an issue. Sure, I wasn't thinking it would be an easy ride with my condition, but seriously, how hard is it to get pregnant?

Extremely, so I discovered over the seven years of trying by ourselves, naturally. You think, *great, we'll just have more sex, that's heaps of fun*, but it was not that much fun after a while, especially when you both come home from work and you're ovulating and you know you have to have sex or it's yet another missed opportunity and, *tick tock*. The clock is ticking honey, so get your gear off and let's get it on. Yeah, it is so easy – NOT!

And everyone says, "Oh just relax and let it happen." Or, "My Aunt Bertha tried for years and suddenly she got pregnant and now has fifteen kids," (not really, just joking). Or they say, "My friend Esmerelda went through IVF and it didn't work, and then a year later she fell pregnant. Just like that."

Baby or Bust

All of these people had kids of their own. I learnt to ignore them. They were trying to be helpful and encouraging but saying that to a 38-year-old woman who had been trying for years, you might see just how relaxed she is not. Especially armed with the knowledge that fertility rates decline at an astronomical speed as you move from your twenties into your thirties. No pressure, honey, just do the deed and hurry up about it!

Why?

When I got older, I really wanted to get married. It was a goal I wanted to achieve. I prayed about it. As I gazed upon or thought about the single males in my life at the time, I did not consider any of them as marriage material. Still, I told God I wanted to get married, that I didn't want to go home alone anymore. I hated that. After a wonderful warm evening chatting, laughing and eating their food (I was young and very happy to receive their hospitality and a decent meal), I would invariably, at some not too late hour, leave my friends and make my way to my little green Datsun Stanza. I would hop in and drive to my little home, a granny flat, small but big enough for me. I put my drum kit in the laundry. There were really good acoustics there for the neighbours to listen to me practising with or without music. No one ever complained, not that I ever knew about anyway.

Anyway, I digress. I'd had enough of being alone. I wanted a male companion to be with, to make love with and wake up with. Less than six months later, I found myself walking across a bridge, as opposed to walking down the aisle, with my fiancé waiting for me in a very warm tuxedo. It was about forty degrees that day, and I was late! My nephew had plucked the head off the rose on the bridesmaid's bouquet, so my mum had to sew it back on, and as we came out of the driveway listening to classical music in my dad's BMW we nearly had a prang. Nothing fazed me that day though; it was the best day!

On arrival, the bridesmaids walked behind me as I strode along. I don't know whose idea it was for the bridesmaid to go first because

The Dreaded Clock

I thought *I am not having that. I've waited long enough, I am going first.* All the while, my dad was by my side saying encouraging things like, "It's not too late, you know, you can still pull out, you don't have to do this," in his jovial fashion. In response, I laughed and walked forward, faster, towards my brand new future.

Once I got married and we settled into married life, well, actually that took about fifteen years, so I'll start this sentence again. Once we had been married for a few years, I began to think about having children. My husband wanted to wait longer than I thought bearable, but eventually we both agreed it was time for us to get pregnant and have a baby. So I went off the pill and we looked forward to the day we would be able to announce we were pregnant to our family and friends.

Instead, nothing happened. That's not exactly true because things happened, both good and bad; our friends were getting married on a regular basis. Before long we had friends who'd married after us pregnant and with babies of their own, and many were younger than me. That hurt so much. It got to the stage where I couldn't handle it when I heard so-and-so was pregnant...again!

At work, in a small country town, several of my colleagues announced on different occasions that they were pregnant. Fortunately for me, I was able to turn away from them before they could see the tears in my eyes. It wasn't that I wasn't happy for them being pregnant. I was just so unhappy that I wasn't. I mean, it's what happens, doesn't it? You get married, you have kids, you raise them, and then they have kids, and you become grandparents. Isn't that the scheme of things? Isn't that the circle of life, as they say?

Why should I be any different?

So I prayed, my friends prayed, and I'm pretty sure some of my family prayed. I talked to God, I begged God. I yelled at God, I beseeched God and tried to bargain with God. Nothing! No answer... no success. Maybe that was the answer.

When I told people we had been trying, their first response was, "Have you considered adoption? Have you thought about being a foster carer?" When people said these things, I really wanted to scream at them. *'You think? No? I sit in a void and don't consider any options but barrenness all of my days!'*

I don't, however, succumb to such revelations of my innermost bitterness. I squish that down, smile benignly and tell them that, "Yes, actually, I have done a bit of research on these options, but you know what? I would really like to have my own children and haven't given up that dream, not yet!" A friend said to me that I should get myself checked out. She said, "You don't want to get to forty and not have kids because you didn't make it happen."

My husband and I did try our hand at being foster carers. It was a rude shock for us to go from being a couple to having a nine-year-old girl living with us full-time overnight. It was a huge challenge as she had behaviours that, while we had completed the foster care training, it didn't *fully* prepare us for what lay ahead. We had two who stayed with us for quite some time. I really loved them and still pray for them and wonder how they are going. We wanted to keep in touch with them, but this wasn't encouraged, and so we lost track of them. When I think of those two it makes me weep as there was so much I wanted to give, but it never worked out the way I hoped.

When we stopped being foster carers we knew we just wanted to have our own children. It was too hard caring for a kid when, due to the establishment's protocol, you had no means to deal with some really intense problems. It was like caring with one hand behind your back. We felt it would be different when you had a child of your own from birth and hoped with all our hearts to have the opportunity.

The Dreaded Clock

We learnt a lot from being foster carers and it would melt my heart when I saw my husband helping them out with homework and school projects and talking to these young people like they were someone important and precious. And that's what they were to us. They were not our children, yet we only wanted the best for them and to support them to blossom and become more confident despite the difficulties they faced. We have photos of us with our foster daughters and memories of laughter, playing games together, cooking dinner and talking about life. This is what being a family is, I thought, and so we continued to fight the battle to have our own baby.

Early on in our marriage, we discussed having kids. It was a no-brainer; of course we both wanted kids, maybe not straight away, but they were definitely on our radar. I was from a family of seven who were doing their part in populating our world very successfully. My mum would say that she just had to go near the bedroom and she'd be pregnant, so fertility was never thought about or discussed in our family. And infertility? Not gonna happen! Not to me.

On our first wedding anniversary in 1995 David bought me a diary in which he'd written the following; "I am glad I am the first to write in it so that every time you go to write in it you can read of how much I love you. I know things have been hard at times but also good. I have come to realise that I am the head of our family of two at the moment, although it is very dear in my heart to make it three very soon with yours and the Lord's blessing."

In February 2005, ten years later, I woke David up during the night, I was in tears and asked him, "Would you be happy if we never had kids?"

"No," he said. Shaking his head, he added, "Well, I guess I'd have to be."

I said, "I'm worried because if we want to adopt we'll have to do something about it soon."

Baby or Bust

Another time, David asked me what would happen if we didn't have kids; I said we would have to have our own adventures.

"Oh, that I might have my request and that God would grant me the thing that I long for," Job 6:8. That's how I felt, and yet the biological clock kept ticking and I was turning thirty-seven in December, and hadn't had sex for ages. I knew being thirty-seven wasn't the end of our chance to have kids, but having a laissez-faire attitude about it was not really helpful.

Looking back, we had checked out our options apart from having our own baby and seriously considered adoption. It was a path we decided not to pursue due to my age and the fact that I had a disability. Not that we saw it as an obstacle, however reading between the lines, trying to explain on paper, the intricacies of a condition that has yet to be diagnosed officially required more effort than the slim hope of success could raise. The costs anticipated just to apply, and subsequent costs of around $30,000 were more than we could afford at that time. Thus it was the path of IVF we were stomping up with hearty enthusiasm.

Or not! I found myself anticipating the IVF wouldn't work and experiencing the grief. Was that stupid? I didn't know. It felt stupid to hope anymore. I felt so down and I couldn't talk to David about it because he couldn't seem to handle my emotions but I couldn't handle my emotions. *Who do I pour out this grief to, who will listen to this sadness?*

> *Walls are for safety, keeping me warm, shutting out the cold, wind and rain. Walls are meant to keep and protect, to shield us from hurts and the pain.*
>
> *The walls loom so large they divide. You in that part of the house as far away from each other as we can be. Smash the walls my love and join me, don't hide.*

The Dreaded Clock

I never anticipated the effect of the intensity of this process on both of us. I probably wouldn't have started it if I knew. Nah that's not true. It was our only hope; we had to give it a try. I knew what I was feeling was different from David's experience. Different but no less intense, frightening or overwhelming. The difficulty was finding the space to hear from each other. Finding the time especially as you go from cycle to cycle with no break and no breakthrough. When do you have fun? How do you just enjoy each other's company when at the back of your mind the baby thing was lurking. Always lurking.

It's like you're on a treadmill, a frenzied, fast-tracking roller coaster that you want to jump off, but you can't because one last try could make all the difference. Yes, that could be the winner. It was the be-all and end-all, the decider if you went out or stayed home. It was the project that impeded other activities—to travel or not. I had to check the calendar, when was I ovulating? When did we need to be having sex?

Once you start you feel there's no choice.

I mean, we both wanted kids so we both had to come to the party, as they say, but as the night progresses and you see your partner's eyes closing, and with that you see your hopes diminishing. You want to scream and say, "No we have to get on with it. Come on, let's just do it; I don't care what you do after that". You watch your hopes fade with the closing of eyes and you can't get upset or angry about it because tomorrow morning we have to do it. Morning arrives and yet another opportunity is wasted and you both go to work, one feeling sad, guilty and useless, the other feeling pissed off and angry and sad because the time is wasted.

That's how it was, if you didn't do *it* on those days, then the chances of falling pregnant were zilch. I remember going to get a blood test on two occasions, sitting weeping while they were taking the blood because I wanted to scream and say, "Why bother, we never did it."

I found going to the clinic rather than pathology less daunting because you got to know the nurses who take your blood, and if you're anything like I was, fearful of needles, then having the same person made it a lot easier. When I first went to get blood tests I would cry after each one of them, I think because I thought it was so futile, but despite the futility I had to do it, I had to try. I had to give my everything. That pressure, along with the fast-ticking biological clock, was the way it was.

Stressed? Yeah, I'd say so, but well-intentioned people would say, "Relax and it will happen." Or they would say, "Just put it out into the universe." Just relax and have sex five times in three days while having injections nightly, taking fertility drugs and sending hormones into racing mode. Both of us were working full-time and studying part-time. Well, we had to work, and while study was an option, we were in the midst of that when we hit the IVF road. I ended up deferring from study as it was just too much.

> *"If another person says to me 'put it out there in the universe' I think I shall tell them where to shove their universe!"*

My family said I was obsessed; they worried about me. My husband said I treated him like a piece of meat. He had his role, and he had to perform many times and once more with feeling, yeah! It's difficult when you are reeling with hormones, working full time, maintaining the home, trying to study, and dealing with a much-loved dog with foot cancer, how can you make room for each other?

It was a weird experience because we both wanted the same thing, and yet getting there, we had different expectations. It was like you were experiencing the most intimate time where you're forced to talk about taboo topics like how do you like sex? How's your libido, and are you in sync? Are you willing to exercise, limit fast food, take vitamins to help promote a healthy pregnancy, stop

The Dreaded Clock

smoking, drink less alcohol, and not go out with mates as much around critical times?

It's a time when you have to face the reality that something in you is not working properly and needs to be fixed before you can reach the goal. Or your partner might be the one with the issue needing to be addressed. Are they willing to do something about it? Are they in denial? You don't have control over that and the frustration of waiting for the other to get sorted, well, let me say a punching bag might be a good idea. Even then, you are keenly aware that even if you jump that hurdle, leap over that obstacle, and cross that barrier there's still no guarantee it will work. You have to face facts and talk about things that you'd really rather not in order to achieve your goal of having that baby.

Amongst all that you have to remember what you love about each other and why you want a child in the first place. You have to understand that the other person is going through their own nightmares and fears and has their hopes and dreams too that they feel are slipping away.

I watched my husband hovering on the periphery, attending appointments wanting to be supportive, not sure what to say or not feeling included. It really made me wonder how the man gets support, how does he fit in, and how does he negotiate this expedition trail where the female is forefront and he is an instrumental, but evidently sideline act? How does he negotiate all the actions and the procedures and feel part of it all. Does he just do what he's told, when he's told, and hope for the best? I know the nurses at the clinic did try to include him. He was, after all the father of the child, and that counts for a lot.

I think there is a lot more support for men now which is fantastic. I have included some resources and contacts at the end of my book for you to check out. David had to play a very active role in all of it because I couldn't do the injections myself. He had to get the alcohol swab, prepare the syringe and then grab my stomach and inject

Baby or Bust

the hormones, sometimes eight times into me a night. Depending on where we were at in my cycle, I would have injections over five nights a month.

There were hiccups with dosages and prescriptions, and sometimes, we had to chase up medications at all hours of the night, thinking we had it sorted, only to find we didn't. One time, because of a mistake in dosage, I had to have six injections to get one full dose instead of just one. My stomach was dotted with needle marks and sore.

Another time I had to get syringes urgently, but the chemist refused to give them to me because they suspected I was a drug user. That went down well, I can tell you. If I told my family or my friends that, they would have laughed a lot because they know my stance on drugs. That put us behind with the process as everything in the lead up and in the process is about timing.

Speaking of timing, David was in a shopping centre where this lady was walking around screaming out, and abusing people. He was super stressed, with lots of responsibility at work, trying to support me and keeping track of the IVF processes. This lady freaked him out a bit and was in his face. People around were looking concerned and she was on the escalator near him, so he tried to get her to calm down. She spat on him. That incident meant that we could not have a cycle for three months while we waited to see if David had contracted Hep C. It was devastating when you felt like you were aging faster by the minute. We cried.

The Dreaded Clock

> "Grief makes you feel physically sick in the stomach and it gives you headaches and it makes you cry so hard that it's the only thing you're conscious of and it wracks your body and leaves it drained. I can't remember not feeling grief. I suppose I can really, like when I was in my 20s before I was married and was an airhead single chick with romantic ideals and dreams."

Try???

Try hard, try harder to achieve the best you can achieve

Keep trying, don't give up, keep believing even through the doubt

Have faith though no evidence is seen

Keep your eyes on God, not the situation

Read the Bible, praise God get close to him, go to Church

Why, why Lord Does it have to be so hard? Am I a screw up?

Do I deserve to not have a child, am I so bad? Help me

Chapter 3

Doing it Naturally

Doing 'it' naturally - The plan was for me to have antenatal tests this week, then have an ultrasound at the end of the my period, which was due on the 8th. On Day 11, have a blood test and have sex when we're told. I had to have two teeth removed because dental problems can stop conception. Bloody *anything* can stop conception. Not having sex at the right time can stop conception, I knew that much.

The deed is done to quote Macbeth. David did the sperm test and dropped the sample off at pathology. He did find it very embarrassing; however, at last it was over and done and now to get the results. The result is that there is a motility issue. It's not an easy thing for a guy to get checked out and then to find that he's got an issue that needs to be dealt with so that he can be a dad. It could be demoralising to discover that your soldiers are not swimming up to speed.

The truth is, it happens, and that is another one of those factors that we have no control over. I'm not saying it's easy for women (I'm very much *not* saying it's easy) but I was happy to get checked out as much as I could to determine whether it was actually possible for me to get pregnant at all.

Once we had the information that yes, actually, there was an issue, then we could deal with it and we did. I imagine it is a difficult thing to face if you're a man and consider virility to be a given. You don't tend to think that you couldn't have a kid if you really wanted to, however, it happens. The good thing is that this news was handled with dignity and an attitude 'of now we know what's going on we can address it and rule it out as a problem'. That was encouraging and gave us hope.

When I went to get sorted, I told the GP (General Practitioner) that I wanted to get pregnant and that I had been bleeding during ovulation. He said, "Well that's not good when you want to get pregnant." I thought, *thank you very much, I'm aware of that*. He added, "You really have to get pregnant soon." What he didn't say was, "You're getting older and the chances of you getting pregnant are getting less and less by the second." I thought, *well we have made a start and identified one issue that can be dealt with through diet and healthy ways of living. Maybe I can do the same.*

Hopeful. I was hopeful. He suggested a gynaecologist and I ended up going to that appointment alone. I do not recommend that. If you're going to go through this process you need to go through it with somebody. You cannot do it alone. It is devastating sitting there, waiting to see this person wondering what they're going to say, what they're going to be able to do for you so that you can make your dream come true.

He said, "Your options are IVF or artificial insemination due to the issue of motility."

I felt like I hit a brick wall—a very hard, cold wall. I felt now God has to do somethingsoon because we really don't want to go down

Doing it Naturally

that track. He said I need to hurry up because my biological clock is ticking very fast. He said, "You have to get pregnant very soon." *Yeah like I don't know that already!*

As I didn't really connect with him and really wanted a female gynaecologist, I kept looking and found another one. This time, I went to a different GP, and when I was speaking to her about it I said, "I need a referral to see this gynaecologist because we're trying to get pregnant."

The GP looked at me and said, "Well you've left it a bit late; you're forty."

I looked at her and said with clenched teeth and hands, "I haven't left it this long. This is how long it's taking."

This time, we both went to the appointment and discussed what options were available. I made it clear that I didn't want to do IVF, I wanted to do what I could and not have to go down that track. Our gynaecologist listened and we set up a plan to start doing it naturally, starting with ovulation induction. This included taking supporting medication and having injections, blood tests and ultrasounds and visiting the clinic regularly. Sounds very natural, doesn't it? Not! The aim was to track my period to get an indication of when ovulation would occur and then let the fun begin.

At ovulation, I would have a blood test at the clinic and wait for a phone call for directions, like when would be the best time to have intercourse. I could be in the middle of appointments or with friends and these phone calls would come through. On answering, someone from the clinic would be saying you have to have intercourse on Tuesday morning and evening, Wednesday morning and evening and Thursday morning. I would remain very neutral in my expression, say, "Thank you very much," and then I would later on call my husband and say, "Okay honey this is happening, this is what we've been told to do, this, we have to do this because now is the time.

Baby or Bust

Please, let's do it." Looking back, I still feel panicky saying all that but that's the way it felt. I mean, we had to go home and have sex which wasn't a bad thing, fun really, however, five times in three days when you're working full-time and studying, and you're doing it because you have to. That is full-on.

Anyway, getting back to the time of ovulation, making love becomes very clinical. What does this mean in reality? It means you both come home from work, perhaps having had a good day, maybe not, but it is on your mind. It's that time again and you have to do it. Maybe you feel like it, maybe you're keen and full of energy. Maybe you feel like a fat blob that is very unsexy, and you're so tired you fall asleep watching TV after eating dinner. There goes that opportunity to get pregnant. Maybe you're feeling anxious that the other person may not want to do it but you think *surely they will try*. Or not.

It was around this time I began having panic attacks where I would just stop breathing, sometimes when I was driving. It was weird and not helpful, but I didn't tell anyone about it at the time. I had to really focus on breathing properly because, at times, I just wouldn't realise I wasn't breathing until I was suddenly gasping for air, like I'd been underwater too long. It took a while to get that sorted, but thankfully I learnt how to manage it with, believe it or not, mindfulness breathing and focussing on things around me that I could see, hear or smell. I say *believe it or not* because people who know me know I would rather go the gym or do some boxing than just sit and breathe. Can't really do those things when you're driving or in a meeting at work, though.

At one point, the receptionist at the clinic was a young man and I can tell you it felt so wrong having him call me and say when and how often I need to have sex in the next few days. He was actually a nice guy, however I felt weird being told by a 22-year-old male when to have sex with my husband. It made me feel uncomfortable. It kinda had that 'I know what you did last summer vibe' ... and he

Doing it Naturally

would know. Nope, I didn't like it. He wasn't there for very long so maybe others felt the same. And yet when a female was calling me and saying how many times and when I needed to have sex, that didn't worry me.

Of course, there was more to it than that. They discovered I had polyps, which hindered pregnancy, so I had to have two lots of day surgeries at different times because new ones replaced the old. This was to eliminate them from the equation. Fun fact – dental health is a significant factor in getting pregnant, so keep flossing, break out the Colgate, and may your McLean's keep showing. I had to get two teeth removed, and if you're scared of dentists like I am, doing that is no picnic. But hey, I was on the way to having a baby. I would do anything to make it happen.

Finally, I was prepared – polyp-free, got rid of decaying teeth, and ready to take the next step. IUI (Intra Uterine Injection), this filled me with so much hope as it bypassed the need for sex at the right time to conceive. It would take the pressure off us both, and hopefully we would be pregnant in the next few weeks. That was the plan and I was excited. Fun fact – polyps apparently can act like an IUD preventing conception, so you really don't want them hanging around.

Adhering to the plan, I had a blood test—they had to do it three times. I had an ultrasound, and I have a good follicle. Anyway, that meant the next day we would do the IUI, and we are fighting all the way. *Oh, happy families! Maybe I can find someone to do some boxing with. I'm so angry. I don't want to do this again. This has got to work because it causes so much conflict between us. I hate it.*

David went to the clinic and did his thing at 9am, then picked me up for our 11am appointment for our first IUI. We didn't get in till 12:15 as they were running late. I got ready and David held the tube of sperm while the nurse inserted the needle tube thing and sucked up the sperm. Then she pushed the needle tube thing up into my uterus, commenting that my mucus was *beautiful* and how it will help the process. Now we just get on with life, go to work, etc, and wait for two weeks. I have a blood test on Thursday and on Sunday a booster injection and another on Wednesday.

I was so hopeful and optimistic, almost to the point of feeling that this was a definite thing. I think I felt that all the hiccups were erased by the procedure. No pressure to perform; just turn up and be there. I mean, it's only a short journey for the sperm to travel, and there's heaps of it. What could possibly go wrong? I was at work and expected good news, I thought that we had overcome the motility issue, the timing issue, the sperm was good, surely it would be successful. It's got to be.

So I was at work and got the phone call. "Sorry, no dice. It's a KFC day." That's what the nurse and I would say. If it was good news, it would mean I was eating salad. If it was negative, then it was KFC. Hmm, it was a KFC day on that day and too many others. I was in shock, more acutely so, due to my over confidence and expectation that this was it. Luckily I had a colleague who I could talk to because she got her ears bashed that day. I was devastated and blamed myself. I said to her, "It's my fault. It's my body that is doing this." And I wept.

That day I learnt a huge lesson—*despite the amazing technology and medical advances we have, I had no control over the outcome.* I was powerless. It hit me that it didn't matter what I did; I couldn't make it happen. I hated that. It meant that I had to trust God knew what he was doing when I didn't have a clue.

> *I don't know what defines me, who am I? At times I feel like I'm a woman waiting to get pregnant so I can start the next phase of my life ie being a mother. But I have been here for over 10 years. Does that mean I'm still back there?*

Doing it Naturally

Please, Lord, I beg you to help me believe in you that this will work out and that I'm not just flogging a dead horse, that you're not letting me go through all the needles for a joke. Help me believe that my husband really does want kids, that he does love me, and that I'm not wasting my time and energy. That the comments of my family and their concern about me being obsessed with having a child is all wrong. That my desire to have a child is not against your will. Help me to believe that I am okay in your eyes and that I'm not a freak who wants to prove she's normal by having a child. I saw my counsellor, and she asked me why I stuff my tears back. I said, "Because I'm afraid I won't stop once I start." And then I said, "I've cried so much what's the point of crying anymore?"

I would like to preface this paragraph by saying: I do not subscribe to animal cruelty at all, those who know how I spoil my pets clearly know that. However, perusing my diary entries during this time, probably over ten years, I can't count the number of times I wrote the phrase *I feel like*. Yep, I felt like I was flogging a dead horse, constantly toing and froing from "I've got to keep doing this while I can" and "I have to do this because that clock is ticking and time is running out." All the while, other thoughts are clashing in my head. *Will this work? Oh no, it didn't work. We should take a break. Or, no, we shouldn't take a break.* Tomorrow night, we have to have sex. Tomorrow morning, we had to have sex. Ironically, our loving feelings were diminished. Now, why would that be? I had a blood test on Monday, and that hurt, I had another one Thursday. The scars are growing on my body. What am I doing? I hope our child will be normal.

All these thoughts going through my mind. I would question my motives: why am I doing this, and why do I want a child, what am I trying to prove, am I trying to prove something? Am I just a woman whose heart's desire is to have a little baby, to have a family? I mean, who has a family of two? That's not the way I thought my family should be. Besides, everyone else in my family was producing beautiful and healthy babies, so why couldn't I have that, too?

Baby or Bust

I remember one time when I was having surgery to get some polyps removed, I was in the waiting room, just waiting to go into surgery when it really hit me about why I was doing this? I just thought, is this morally, ethically, right for me to be doing this because I have a disability? Does that mean that our child would have a disability? Does that mean that I would be putting another person in the position of having a disability because of me? It really made me think about what my motives were about having a child. Do I just want to be like my brothers and sisters? No. I really, really wanted to be able to say to my husband, "Here is our child, our little baby." I thought, well, hey, I have a disability and I have the best life. I would make sure our children would have the best whatever the situation. Just like my mum and dad did for me.

At one point in the midst of all this I said to my husband that he should leave me and find another wife. Find a woman who can have kids. I'm not really sure what he thought when I said that to him, but I was serious. That was a very intense conversation in which my husband made it very clear that he was staying regardless of whether we could have kids or not. He loved me for me. Hearing that was pretty amazing.

Speaking of doing it naturally, one time David had to give me eight injections because we had the wrong measurements so we had to make up the Mls. It was to make the egg healthy. That was scary, I was upset, tense, and stressed but got over it. The whole thing was a drama that I was already over and didn't want to make each step of the journey even more of a melodrama.

Another time, doing it naturally. I think it was hysteria, I was tired. David gave me the injection and I started to laugh. This made him laugh too. I mean, he was sticking a needle into my stomach and there I was cracking up, laughing, which made the muscles tense up nice and tight, and it hurt like hell but we were still laughing. Moments like those makes marriage feel great!

Chapter 4

The Harvest

I remember the day when we had to make a decision about going the whole hog. We had tried other fertility treatments to no avail and all we were left with was in vitro fertilisation (IVF). We were reviewing the processes that we had been doing over several years with the gynaecologist. These included natural cycles, intra uterine injection (IUI), and Intracytoplasmic Sperm Injection (ICSI) which is when the sperm is injected dirIctly into the egg. What more could we do? There was nowhere else left to go. I looked at my husband and told him that I really didn't want to do IVF. The gynaecologist said, "We have done everything else we can do, there are no other options available." I paused mid-thought and we agreed that we had come this far so we may as well keep going. We had to keep trying while we could. We were doing a lot of the procedures anyway, or so I thought.

If someone asked me if I ever thought I would consider IVF as a means to have a baby, I would never have said yes. I have had lots of medical treatments and had many nightmares of being chased by matrons with injections just for me. The idea of intensifying the level of hormone injections, as well as having a clearer grasp of the impact of hormone treatment on my physical and mental health, did not appeal to me. I was scared, I wanted to have a baby so desperately but please can it be as natural as possible. Consenting to IVF meant I gave up that ideal. I physically couldn't do it naturally.

When you are undertaking IVF the process is explained many times but for those who are interested in a very simplified version of the process of IVF, it includes the following:

- Ovulation induction – This is where you get pumped with loads of fertility drugs to stimulate the release of one or more eggs from the ovary. In my case , a lot more. Blood tests, injections on certain days of cycle, ultrasounds. A variety of drugs that make you feel like grazing, that's what the side effect list said. If grazing is eating whatever is available slowly and methodically and wondering why you can't stop, then I grazed regularly and thoroughly.
- Egg retrieval – Harvesting. This requires day surgery where the eggs are collected to be fertilised and stored for future use.
- Fertilisation – The eggs are fertilised with sperm ready for transfer. Embryos may be viable or not, and sometimes viable ones degrade when being thawed (I think there's a technical term for it, but you get it). So you might start with ten and end up with six viable for example. It costs money for storage, which we paid monthly.
- Embryo transfer – This occurred at the clinic and was painless. Some people choose to use multiple embryos and can end up having twins or triplets or more. We chose two for our first transfer. This is where pessaries are introduced. These are important as they assist in the production of progesterone, which assists in supporting the embryos to develop.
- Two-Week Wait – The longest two weeks ever…

The Harvest

Having made that decision to proceed to the IVF stage we needed to get $5000 by the next week. We borrowed $4000 from my in-laws which was incredible that they did that for us. We paid them back and were able to save for our next round, just in case the current one didn't work.

All I wanted to do was be free to be me, and to dance, and love life, and live it to the fullest. To sail with the wind in my hair, the sun shining softly on my face and the crystal clear sea water nearby. Yeah, I think that meant I just needed to escape from reality for a while, and I needed a boat. Not a bigger one. Just a boat.

I spoke to the nurse who said we need to get started on the 16th of October if we want to do a November cycle, which meant that by December, I should be pregnant. I said to David, "If this doesn't work we're going overseas." At this time, our dog was in pain, our pet mouse was sick, and David and I were fighting about money or just about anything. He was worried about his job and me, and we were not talking. Great way to start a family!

Apart from all that, things were going according to plan. I had deregulated with help from some medication, bringing my hormones to a pre-menopausal state. I had a blood test last week, then Tuesday again, as well as an ultrasound. I planned to take a day off work for day surgery for egg pick up on Friday the 13th—don't you just love that date! Then two to five days later we would go back for the injection of two fertilised embryos and subsequent pessaries up my rear end to assist the process. Sounds so elegant and lovely.

You have to realise that the drugs they give you during infertility treatment are pretty heavy-duty, and I was on very high doses. But you don't think of that when you're just trying to get pregnant. You just do what you're told to do when you're told to do it because the target is pregnancy no matter what. i.e. baby or bust.

Baby or Bust

We were both working and studying whilst going through this process' I don't think that was the best way to do it. However, the reality is you have to pay for it somehow, and you still have to eat. The study got put off and what should have taken four years ended up taking eight to achieve. Anyway, hindsight is just annoying, so there's no point in going there. In my diary, I wrote

September 2009 Ultrasound 16 follicles of good size, looks like it's all systems go. Injection of Estrogen 7000 plus. Have to continue gonal f today and tomorrow as well as nasal spray, and on Wednesday we do the trigger of 10,000, then on Friday I go to hospital get sedated and the eggs are taken out of me. 2-5 days later embryo's inserted . David has to provide good quality sperm on Friday. I feel like it's all going brilliantly

12/11 feels uncomfortable - tiring. Ultrasound revealed 16 follicles so my tummy is full and I feel windy and fat. I wonder if that's how you feel when you're pregnant. It's not a pleasant way to be.

It's all happening tomorrow. David asked me if I was feeling nervous. I'm not really however I will be glad to be free of all these eggs in me and for it to be over, well, I still have to have pessaries, injections and blood tests so that might take a while.

The operation went well. In the waiting room I sat thinking is this madness, me trying to have children. Once again, I had all these doubts, yet I stayed and walked in and had it done, not that I had much choice at that stage. They got nineteen eggs. No wonder I felt so stuffed. Eight are mature, seven are likely to become mature and four are unusable. Sperm quality is good. It was a kind of surreal experience. The doctor was happy with the outcome and it looks like on Wednesday I go in and get fresh fertilised embryo's put in me. On tthe 18th November I went into clinic and got two embryos put in. The rest will be frozen for future use if it doesn't work this time. Now I need to keep pessaries going and blood tests to check progesterone levels.

The Harvest

The procedure to get embryos placed was painless and easy and I felt very confident when I left, a bit tired but good. I had to be positive. I really thought this would work.

What are the Odds?

I woke up Friday morning, and my arms and legs felt as heavy as lead as I shuffled down the hallway. Something was crook in Tullarook, as the saying goes. I had a shower, let Hawkeye out, got dressed, tried to eat but only because I forced myself to. I could barely move without pain. It was hard to breathe and my stomach felt as if it was pressed up against my ribs. A thought occurred to me. Hyperstimulation! I phoned the clinic and was told to get to Emergency as it sounded like a mild case of hyperstim. David took me straight away.

When we got to Emergency, they let me in immediately, got me a gown and a bed. I spent the day there getting blood tests and going over our IVF, etc, with several doctors. One doctor explained hyperstim to me, and I asked how long I needed to stay, her response was: "Until you get better." She said, "If you don't get treatment now you'll end up in ICU." Another doctor said it takes one or two weeks. This is particularly referring to my belly, which was swollen, so I looked very pregnant. *At least*, I thought to myself, *I now have an idea what I'll look like!* We had to keep reinforcing the point that I am potentially pregnant as I have two embryo's inside of me and thus any treatment prescribed needs to take that into account. They'd come this far, surely God wouldn't allow their efforts to be trashed. I discovered later that apparently hyperstimulation doesn't affect the embryos, I am not sure whether I believe that but, *hey, I'm not a doctor.*

I was in the ED for a few hours before transferring me to the maternity ward which I shared with a young lady. *I don't know if I mentioned it, but I felt so bloated, and you know what that means? If you don't, let me explain.*

Baby or Bust

I could barely move by myself. I was unsteady and thus needed assistance to transfer from one bed to the bed in the ward. Just picture this (or not) I am wearing a white hospital gown with only knickers underneath. As I moved, and I mean only ever so slightly, sounds erupted from nether regions. Places and sounds that ladies don't discuss and never admit to being responsible for. I tell you every move I made, I farted loudly and sometimes even tunefully. If there was a Guinness Book of Records for the longest passing of wind, I would be a serious contender. As I was in a lot of pain at the same time, I kinda was more amused than embarrassed because I had absolutely no control over it. I bet the wardsman were happy to get me into my bed so they could get the heck out of there.

Once settled in my bed, it continued. I couldn't sneeze without pain or unleashing more gas. My room mate had to suffer the sounds of release many times over the first few days. At first I would apologise but after a while I didn't bother. Fortunately, she was a good humoured person with compassion.

I had regular urine tests as they were concerned about my liver and kidney function. My urine was browner than I had ever seen it, which freaked me right out. I grabbed bottles of water and consumed them with vengeance.

We had to remind people that we had embryos inside me and to consider that when taking X-rays. I also had to get the nurses to help with pessaries to sustain their viability. Man, this IVF stuff is really invasive. It's bad enough when you have to do that yourself, or your partner does it, but when you have to get a different nurse each time. All the time I felt like they were thinking, *Why are you bothering to go along with this charade – they're dead!*

It was demoralising. They never said anything and were very professional, but I felt the vibe. Or maybe it was me thinking that there's no way the embryos could survive this ordeal and yet I could not let it go. I had to do anything to help if I could, and that

The Harvest

was in my power, therefore, I got them to do it. It was hard keeping intrusive thoughts out of my head.

As the swelling wasn't reducing the doctors were considering a procedure that required sticking a needle into my vagina. I am not sure what that procedure was officially labelled, but in my mind it was the *Not Gonna Happen* procedure, and I prayed for God to do something so I didn't have to endure it. They came to collect me so they could do it, even got me into the procedure room, but when they did the assessment, it appeared that my system was righting itself naturally and the swelling was reducing. Praise God. I didn't need to have it. It was a victory ride back to my room, at least until the nurse who was taking me back said that hyperstimulation can reduce the quality of the eggs. I just couldn't bear to hear that, it was my turn to go *lalalala*.

As a part of the IVF treatment, I was meant to have a booster injection on day five after embryo transfer (it's a shot to boost the embryo growth and development). As I was in hospital we had to consult with doctors there who basically said that if I had it, they would not be responsible for the outcome as they felt the risk was too high for me. Essentially, having the injection could potentially help the embryos if they were still alive, but it might kill me, or at the very least do a lot of harm. What a choice.

We did not know whether the embryos had survived the onset of hyperstimulation or not. We tried to make contact with my IVF doctor and see if they could communicate with the treating doctors at the hospital. However this attempt only highlighted the fractures in our system as because I was in hospital, there would be no consultation with outside practitioners. Didn't seem right to me and left us unable to ask the questions we wanted to ask to be able to make an informed decision.

After another heated discussion with David and with the doctors, I decided not to have the booster shot. I can't tell you the devastation

Baby or Bust

I felt as I made that decision. Any hope I had for those two precious potential human beings was decimated. I still cry when I think about it. I felt very alone. Despite this and the sinking feeling of futility, I persisted with pessaries to maintain my progesterone levels to help keep them safe, just in case.

It probably would help if I explained what exactly hyperstimulation syndrome is and how to check symptoms, keeping in mind that I am not a medical person at all. It's a condition that occurs when you have too much of the pregnancy hormone HCG in your system. As I was in the process of harvesting and wanting to generate a decent amount of eggs I was prescribed a high dose. This overstimulated my ovaries, resulting in swelling and leaking fluid. This can also affect other organs, such as the kidneys and liver, and potentially cause blood clots and dehydration, hence the brown urine and my strong desire for water.

It is not something you want to go through. IVF is hard enough without that. Fortunately, the odds of getting hyperstimulation are pretty low. I recently did a brief check and an article published in 2015 by Obstetrics and Gynaecology Internatonal, stated that the incidence of moderate to severe OHSS is between 3.1 and 8% of in vitro fertilisation (IVF) cycles'. As you have regular blood tests and ultrasounds during IVF treatment, these can alert you if things are going that way, thus it can be picked up early and managed. While the risk of hyperstimulation was told to me at the beginning, I didn't fully appreciate the reality that it actually *could* happen to me. I mean, what are the odds, eh? In retrospect, if I had been more aware of the symptoms maybe I could have avoided it and saved us a lot of angst.

Lesson learnt – review patient information sheet, check out symptoms and let your clinician know as soon as possible if you're experiencing any of them. I don't mean to be an alarmist, but if you talk about it with them and your symptoms are nothing serious, that is great. If you talk about it and it turns out that it is something, well at least you caught it and can deal with it.

The Harvest

During this time, my mum came and stayed and visited me in the hospital. It was such a blessing to have her with me even though I could barely get out of bed. My mum and I go way back as far as hospital stays go, and it reminded me of my many hospital stints when I was younger. Having her there at this time was special even though I couldn't tell her all the stuff that was going on. I couldn't tell anyone. My dad and my sisters, and I even think my brothers checked in on me via phone, which meant a lot. They were all worried about me. I was worried about me but more worried about our little ones. My friend patted my bloated tummy and prayed for them.

One person I didn't know well from church came to visit, but I had to end that visit rather quickly as my gas issues hadn't quite resolved and that was something I really didn't want to share. It was funny, though, and made me laugh to myself. I'm saying *'thanks for your visit'*, and he's, like *'oh well I'm not in a hurry'*, and I'm saying *'well I need to rest up now and thanks, see you another time'*. He probably thought I was a bit rude, but the way I see it, I think I saved him. As soon as he left, I was in that bathroom and it wasn't pleasant.

I spent six days in hospital and was discharged on the day of our 15th wedding anniversary. I remember walking to the car after leaving the hospital, feeling the fresh air and sunshine, glad to be out but feeling exhausted. It was a rather subdued event despite David trying hard to make it special and Hawkeye's joy to have me home again.

David had bought us both cards and gifts for each of us to give to one another. We wrote in each other's card at the same time and exchanged gifts. He'd put a lot of time and effort into acknowledging that this year, on this day in particular, it was important to remember us as a couple. That meant a lot to me, especially when we found out a few days later that we lost the two babies. He reminded me that we are a family, children or no children.

Baby or Bust

So I sit in my bed

Let the tears fall from my head

The sobs that shake my soul

Threaten to rock my body whole

I recall with such clarity & delight

Having my baby in me, for whom I'd fight

Then cruelly having to say goodbye

Without a reason, never knowing why

Alas little one, here for a time

You'll always, always be mine

Chapter 5

Positively Pregnant

Everyone knows that the object of the IVF process is to get pregnant and have a baby. That's what we were aiming for! And yet, when it actually happened, I found it hard to believe. It was like I was on this impossible mission that was doomed from the start and yet, it worked. I got pregnant. Whoa, now to recalibrate that negative vibe.

It had been a difficult year because in February, we had had to say goodbye to Hoolihan, our 12-year-old rottweiler, who was a standing member of our little family of two dogs, two mice, and two birds. She was the gentlest dog with a happy nature and part of my keeping well strategy while in the midst of the IVF fog. She would join me in karaoke, singing Abba and Queen songs together. She would start howling with me, I'm not sure whether it was because I sounded bad or if she just liked the music. Her death left me with a hole in my support system and Hawkeye, our Australian Terrier, without his best mate.

Baby or Bust

Not long after Hooli died, our two pet mice, Jindie Brie and Colby, died, which added to our grief. Yes, I know mice aren't always a favourite, our neighbour was terrified of them, but to us, they were so cute and lovable. Their dying added to our loss and reminded us of how many babies we had lost.

I was pregnant in June 2010. I remember the day well. I had a blood test before I went to work and my usual nurse wasn't there as she was sick. I stayed in the office as I found that if things didn't work out, I could manage my emotions sufficiently by using the toilet to hide in and having tea with sugar (which I don't usually do) to help with the shock.

This day was different. I got a call from the nurse who said she was glad she didn't do the blood test because she was unwell. She said it a few times before I twigged. She meant that she was glad because she wouldn't want to put me at risk because I was pregnant. I had to get her to spell it out for me. I was stunned. I left work in a daze. I called David and we agreed to meet for lunch in the city near where he worked. I was so excited!

We met and we sat down in the café. I scanned the room for waiters. All clear, none visible so I took his hand and told him the nurse had phoned me and told me I was pregnant. Just as I finished saying it a waiter appeared out of nowhere with menus. Really? He got the vibe and made a quick exit. David looked stunned. He swallowed and said, "Can you repeat that?" I was happy to say, "Yes, we are going to have a baby!" And then he asked if I was sure.

And yet another waiter appeared. Evidently, the service is very good at this café. David asked him to give us a minute, it was funny, you know, like in the movies, the timing was so bad. We ordered him a champagne and me an orange juice. We were thrilled and excited and fearful all at once. He said, "Now I am really freaking out. We were going to be parents – Mummy and Daddy – us!" Oh, what a feeling!

Positively Pregnant

We called our family members, there's a lot on my side. The news was received with joy and concern from my family. They knew what we had already been through and only wanted the best for us but... I could tell. Underneath they were worried. My brother-in-law Darren said, "It's about time!" which David and I had a chuckle over. I don't know that he realised how hard we had been trying.

Despite the concern, I took this win and was determined to get as much out of it as possible. When you do IVF and become pregnant the embryo is said to be one month along from transfer date. This meant that I was one month pregnant for real and experiencing pregnancy symptoms like increasing breast size which was a bonus and a half, I actually felt like I had some!

I could no longer bear to drink coffee; I couldn't even stand the smell. My body felt like it was zinging; ecstatic and sexy, an amazing feeling that I relished and allowed myself to revel in as I didn't know how long it would last. I hoped, we hoped, actually everyone who knew us hoped and prayed it would work out. My dad asked if I was going to be in hospital, and at the time I thought that was odd, but on reflection it was actually a valid question.

We anticipated this absolute miracle to be realised in February 2011. One Saturday we went out for breakfast to bask in the joy, the cautious hopeful excited joy that we would be having our own little child. We talked about what I should and shouldn't eat (I was eating fresh white bread with cream and sugar – it was something I had when I was a kid, and during this time I craved it), and then we came to our favourite topic, picking names.

We had a lot of fun going through ideas and what would work if our baby was a boy or if our baby was a girl. I didn't care either way, I was just so ecstatic that I was actually pregnant. This was happening and it was happening to me. It was my turn. I felt so overjoyed to be pregnant after such a tumultuous journey. My body was changing and I loved the feeling of being pregnant. Me!

Baby or Bust

I thanked God for the opportunity to be able to have a little baby growing inside of me, it was absolutely astounding. I wanted to eat healthy, get exercise (but not too much), and rest.

I called my family and my mum called my oldest brother, he responded with: "Oh ****" probably not the reaction I was going for, but, hey, it was appropriate for him. My family were excited but scared for me. They were scared because I had a disability' and I didn't even know what this would do to my body, and they were scared if something went wrong.

If they were scared, I was terrified. My Gynaecologist saw me waiting to get a blood test one morning and she looked at me and said I wish I could just wrap you up in cotton wool and keep you so safe until you have this baby. I looked at her and knew I really wanted to do that. Just hide and let my baby grow and develop inside me. Alas, the world of domesticity, study, and work and life beckoned. I thought I could do it all. Well, I did take it easy to some extent but mostly kept doing what I usually did; after all, pregnancy was not an illness, and so I thought I should get on with it all like everyone else did.

I continued to have blood tests every three days as directed to ensure that my progesterone levels were high enough to sustain the pregnancy. It was the same nurse who called me a few weeks later and said they were worried because the HCG levels were not high enough, they weren't going up. By that time, they should've been 5000, and they were only 480, and the nurse said, "Sorry it looks like you will miscarry." After this call I put the phone down, it was a landline phone, and I was at work. I left without a word.

I walked out of the office in shock and ran into a client who wanted to see me even though we didn't have an appointment. "I can't see you, I'm sorry, I have to go now," I said in a voice that didn't seem to be mine. It was like I was in a dream, a haze with nightmarish qualities, and I wanted to run from but it clung to me like glue.

Positively Pregnant

I don't recall how I told David, I think the nurse phoned him. I told my boss and said we were *getting out of Dodge and going to Melbourne for a week*.

We visited my mum on the way and stayed a night. We took our little dog Hawkeye with us as we needed him at this time. I blabbed on to Mum who was understandably upset. The nurse who told me I was about to miscarry had said to me that she was so sorry and that she felt that this is worse than having a negative result. I vehemently said, "Absolutely not." Those weeks of being pregnant were amazing and I feel abundantly blessed that I was able to have that time. Not every woman gets that, and I knew a few who have tried so hard. Sure it hurt like hell, but the experience of having a little baby inside of me was miraculous and joyful. That baby was loved and I do not regret having the opportunity to experience pregnancy for an instant.

When we arrived in Melbourne my sister was there with her partner. We were in the kitchen talking, and I was explaining what had happened, and her partner said, "Yes, it's hard but you just have to get over these things and move on." I looked at him in horror, wanting to punch him in the face. I was in the process of miscarriage, losing my baby, a baby we had fought for, for so long and so hard. I could not form the words to speak and just looked away.

Just an FYI for what not to say. I know he didn't intend for it to come across that way but it hurt.

We stayed there for a few days, my sister Sam supporting me as the inevitable happened while hanging out with them and my nephews, doing everyday stuff like shopping and going to watch my nephew play in a footy match. Probably all good things to do to keep myself busy and give time to process what was happening without having to work, cook, clean or think straight. I had some pain, but it wasn't bad, I felt like it should be worse. It was weird waiting and even weirder seeing what could have been our baby.

Baby or Bust

On the way home we stopped at a service station to get some breakfast. I walked into the toilet stall and the toilet paper got stuck in the dispencer, and I tried to get it but couldn't. I punched it and swore at it loudly, I didn't break it, thankfully, but I'm pretty sure everyone heard the commotion. Oh, man, it makes me laugh thinking about it because I stopped *bazaking* (as I say), flicked my not-so-long blonde hair as models do, wiped my eyes and walked out as if nothing happened. I mean, who was making that racket seriously, wasn't me. A lady looked at me and I just smiled calmly, washed my hands and walked out. Very therapeutic. Not sure if I would promote this strategy because you could do damage and that would not be helpful.

I remember lying in bed staring at the smoke alarm for ages, not moving, just thinking or not thinking, trying not to feel. One night I woke up crying, David held me. I said, "I feel like it's a cruel joke God played on us. To let us have a glimpse of the dream and then take it away, how cruel is that?" Many nights I woke up crying. It's just a way to let the grief out even though I kinda thought I was crying enough in my waking hours.

We shared our news that we were pregnant with a few select friends, not many as it was early days and we wanted to be sensible and realistic. (Not really, I wanted to shout it out to everyone) I remember sitting in our friends' house and telling them we were going to have a baby. I felt like I belonged to a new club. The parents-to-be club, the mum's club. It was like I was now included in a whole different world that I couldn't reach without a child. I loved the feeling. It gave me confidence and joy and excitement. I was looking forward to the challenge of being a mum.

I remember the night it happened. I woke up suddenly. I know that sounds dramatic, but it was abrupt. I felt different somehow and a sense of unease. I couldn't tell anyone, couldn't say the words out loud. I could hardly bear to think them. Something was wrong, I felt it but couldn't explain it, and to admit it out loud. No that would be too much. I had lunch with a friend that day and still told her I was pregnant, she was thrilled and I tried to enjoy the moment but I was worried. A week later we were told we were miscarrying.

I didn't want to tell people that I was having a miscarriage as it felt like I was admitting defeat. I questioned whether I did something wrong, did I not deserve to have a child? I felt like I missed a memo somewhere saying this is how to do this and I didn't do the right thing. The pain got worse, and I was on Panadeine Forte, bleeding and cramping steadily. I wanted it all out of me so I wouldn't need a DMC or curette. I didn't know whether I wanted to do this again. We still had four embryos left, so four more chances...if we wanted to take them.

I couldn't think that far into the future. It was too overwhelming but I tried to make lists of things that I needed to do to help me achieve at least something each day and to rein in the catastrophising thoughts swirling in my head. My diary records that: *Tomorrow we are going out for breakfast to celebrate David's birthday. I was so looking forward to him turning thirty-six and becoming a daddy.*

I blamed myself and my body, and I didn't think I was far off the mark. My body physically just couldn't sustain a pregnancy. That's the way it is and I have accepted that. The doctors could not find any reason why I couldn't conceive and follow through with pregnancy. According to the clinical team, everything looked perfect. I have learnt that unexplained inability to have children is actually a thing. It happens to people, not just me. Mind you, knowing that doesn't make it easier to deal with, you still gotta go through the darkness to get to the other side.

I kept taking the medications and still hoping that they were wrong, the levels would increase again and our baby would be okay. The nurse said, "Keep doing it and have a blood test in two days and then we'll see."

Baby or Bust

"Should I keep doing everything? Like is there any point?" I asked.

"Probably not," she replied, but I did anyway because I was determined to help my baby. We received a letter from the clinic asking me to come in for our first ultrasound. It arrived the day we discovered we were miscarrying. I kept it as a reminder that, yes, it was really real. We were pregnant. I had a little baby inside of me.

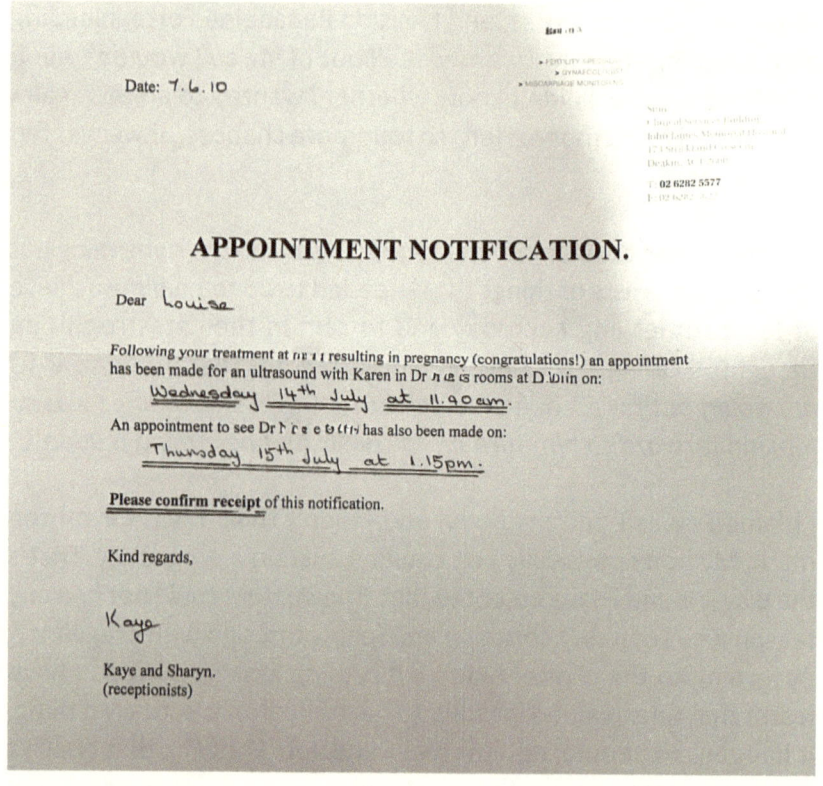

I remember one night we were in bed and my husband was listening to music, he gave me the headphones and said, "Just listen." He played *It's my Life* by *Bon Jovi*, and I burst into sobbing, messy tears because I didn't want to be held back by my grief I just wanna live while I'm alive. Yeah, inspiration and encouragement and an outlet for my grief. Thank you, Bon Jovi – I'm still a fan today.

Positively Pregnant

Each time we did a cycle we were given a photo of the embryo and we would take it home. It's pretty amazing when you see it because it's incredible that from this very tiny thing (yeah, science was never my thing) comes a human being. Take a look at the photo below.

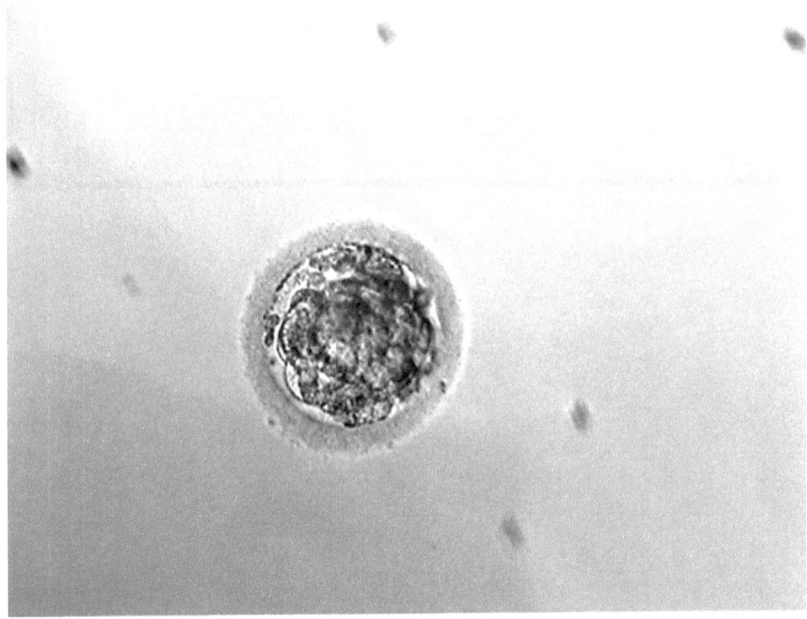

I have kept all the photos of our potential babies always full of hope that they would become our dream come true. Why do I still have them? I guess it's an important part of my life that they were the focus for so long and thus too precious to discard.

Baby or Bust

To mourn the loss and feel the grief

Trudge through the darkness

Seeking some relief

I cannot change it though how hard I try

I felt your life inside me and I felt you die

Recognising The Anticipated Date of Birth

On this day, I purchased a bunch of flowers. The flowers were gerberas, lots of pink ones with a few other colours to represent our other babies. I really thought our baby would be a girl. I got dressed up, put on makeup and drove down to the pond near our house and sat on the grass and wrote the following poem crying as I did. Just for a change.

The Birthday Party

Today we should be celebrating with joy with streamers balloons, family laughter. Lots of gifts for you - my baby. Instead I am here alone wishing you were with me today, I can't understand why you're not but that's the way it is.

I wore a dress for this occasion; I believe you were going to be a girl and chose you a pink gerbera, it's pretty and fine. And I want to keep it as long as I can but I won't because today is special, today is the day I let you go. I let you go and know you're safe with God.

I want you to know that I loved it when you were growing inside of me. I was so thrilled and excited like never before. And I knew the instant when something had gone wrong I know you fought it, but God had other plans. For you and for me.

I'm happy you're safe from this world but so sad it hurts me physically. Yet I have to trust God knows what he's doing. Anyway I'm going to say goodbye now, although I don't want to go. Know that David & I loved you and wanted you so much. We look forward to seeing you in Heaven. In the meantime Hooli will look after you and I'm sure the mice Jindi Brie & Colby will play with you and you can listen to Miracle, No Name and Bluebird chirp merrily.

Goodbye my littlest Poppet,
love from your mummy — me

Positively Pregnant

After writing the above I took the flowers and placed them in the water. I stood and watched their slow progression as they moved along with the current. To me it was symbolic of my starting to let go of the grief from losing our baby. I did this for several years and I always bought a variety of colours to represent the different babies we may have had over the years. I didn't always go to the pond but had flowers in my home around that time to remind me of the joy that I had being pregnant and being thankful for it. And yes, I do shed a tear or two each year. What a surprise!

Lost dreams

Lost dreams where do they go

To the bin I really don't know

Lost hope when does it leave

When do I really start to grieve

Lost time can I ever get it back

Will I make it up do I have the knack

Lost friendships were they even real

Don't know where they went nor what I feel

Lost babies whose presence I so long

Though without I struggle hard to be strong

Lost passion for anything with meaning

Saying and doing things that are demeaning

Lost battles I don't want to fight anymore

I just shrug and no longer care what's in store.

Chapter 6

The Angry Ant

Angry! Yep. I punched my punching bag and swore my head off. I was so angry I was shaking. I was feeling like a fool for even entertaining the idea that I could have a baby. And I was furious at God for not taking the dream away. David came out and saw me pelting the living daylights out of the punching bag and said I was freaking him out. "Well, get out then!" I screamed. "Don't see me like this." I was livid and violently swinging punches. My head hurt, and felt like it would explode.

Anger is ugly. It was beating at me. I wanted to work through it and get it out of my system. Boxing has always been a good way to do it, I just didn't want to hurt myself in the process.

I was so upset I lay on the bed and cried. It's like some little thing happens and I crack up, feel like it's hopeless and feel overwhelmed and like I don't want to be here anymore. I didn't know where I wanted to be, just that I wanted to be away. I think that's called running away! But you can't run away from yourself, and you can't run away from your grief. I felt like it was my fault David and I couldn't have kids.

Baby or Bust

I felt like yelling at my brother-in-law who was visiting us for Christmas, one I had worked so hard to make perfect: "Do you realise how hard it is to have you waltz over, get married and have a child in the space of eighteen months—eighteen-*bloody*-months—when David and I have been married for seventeen years and lost so many babies that I can't count them anymore. And if I seemed a bit snappy cut me a little slack." It was a hard time because our baby would have been born a few months before their baby who was also staying with us. Fair dinkum, I was a bit touchy, can you blame me, really? I know he didn't mean anything by it and he wasn't wrong but I just wished hecould have been a bit more caring for what we had been through.

There were many times I felt I couldn't cope with my friends or work colleagues getting pregnant and announcing the happy news at morning tea. I was so glad my back was turned when one told us all as it gave me a moment to get my game face on and turn around and pretend to be happy for her after all my years of trying to get pregnant. One time I found myself in the position of being in the workplace with three colleagues who were pregnant at the same time. If my baby had lived he or she would have been baby number one for the year. Instead, we didn't get a mention because it didn't happen.

My reaction when a close colleague gave me the heads up that she was pregnant via IVF was to swear profanely, something I didn't normally do, but unhappily it had become more commonplace for me in the last few years. All I could think of was how am I going to cope with seeing her growing belly, and under my sunglasses, tears ran down my cheeks.

One girl had been pregnant two years previously and talked about it incessantly. It was an exciting time for her. For me, it meant leaving the tea room and dining alone, especially now that she was pregnant with her second child. I could have screamed. The others had had miscarriages earlier in the year, so I hoped it would work out well for them. I only wanted the best for them all, but I just didn't want to be around them. The very thought of watching them grow devastated me. It isn't that I'm not happy that they're pregnant. I'm just pissed off at the world, God, everyone because it's not me. Why not me? I cried to God why do I have to be confronted by three freaking women who's very presence says I've got what you'll never have haha. These women have trials and experiences of getting pregnant and staying that way. I know that in my head, but honestly, how can I bear it? if I see a pregnant woman, I can't look at her. I walk away pretending not to see her. It's nothing to do with them personally. It's my defence mechanism kicking in on high gear.

> *You know I can track my cycle almost to the hour of ovulation? That's what five years of IVF treatment will do to you. Even when I'm not interested I still know...*

My younger sister Susie came to Canberra with her boyfriend and Mum to stay the weekend. This was a big deal to me. She and Mum were in the kitchen with me while I was preparing dinner. Susie said she had something to tell me and I knew straight away what it was. I went cold inside and said as I turned to her, "You're pregnant," before bursting into sobbing tears. It was what I dreaded. My little sister having a baby before me. It should've been me, not her, I thought. I'm older, and getting *too* old. I'm married. I'm the one who has actually been in a stable relationship for the past twelve years, and she says she's pregnant.

Susie has two kids now and for the second one I didn't bat an eyelid. Once, twice, thrice, whatever. But I'm glad I was not bitter about it, ha. Looking back I wonder how she felt about my reaction because it was *her* good news and something to be very happy about. I was so engrossed in my unhappiness that I wasn't there for her at all.

Baby or Bust

My diary entry stated: *Well I am happy for my sisters but what do I do? I feel there's no hope for me in this area and I can't see any hope in the future. Is the dream dead? Can it die and still be resurrected? My hopes have been smashed to smithereens, and I'm bordering on the brink of disappointment growing to cynicism and resentment. Don't want to go there because if there's no hope what is there?*

And shaken, I was so shaken when Susie told me she was pregnant. My little sister was having a baby, and my other younger and older sisters have all had babies or were on the way, and me with no kids. Susie said, "It's just not fair." I just wanna move on go and get a full-time job and just live to the fullest. I don't want to be like this anymore.

In June 2006, I listed the pros and cons of fostering, and adoption in Australia (somewhat ambitious) and overseas, and considered them all. I phoned several organisations about adoptions and discovered we fill in the expression of interest form and go to a seminar, get assessed and approved and then after six months we could be on the way to adopting a two-year-old child from either China, the Philippines, Ethiopia, Latvia or Thailand.

Well, as usual, nothing was easy. It was going to cost us roughly $30,000 to adopt a child. David said that if I was serious about adoption I really needed to be seeking full-time employment with good wages. So here I was again, on the brink of hope versus despair. A profound sense of hopelessness when I thought about the obstacles needing to be overcome, and not only in the process but in myself and David and our marriage. It felt all too hard I didn't think we would be adopting a baby.

During this time, I heard on the grapevine that someone we knew got his girlfriend pregnant, and what do you know? They had an abortion! My sister told me this so casually I could have reached through the phone and punched her in the face. She told me like it was no big deal. For me, how women can have an abortion is beyond my comprehension. Having been pregnant for seven weeks, feeling so different, and seeing my body changing. How can any woman say it's their choice and body and say it's okay? For me, it's too horrific to believe. With all the contraception we have and the blurb that goes on about both parties being sexually responsible. I say there's not a lot of room for excuses for unwanted pregnancy to occur. I know there's a lot more to say on both sides of the story, but I don't give a shit about the other side of the story. This is my story if you don't like it or agree with what I'm saying, that's okay. I don't care. Don't read it.

One evening I was checking out Facebook and discovered that my sister-in-law was a few months pregnant, and not one of my family had given me the heads up. Finding out on a stupid social media site is not the way this happy news should be told. I went from hang on, that's my sister-in-law. Hang on, she's pregnant? Nobody told me. I flew out of my office and into the lounge room where my husband was enjoying his TV show, however, on my stormy entrance he sat up quickly and braced himself. It was almost comical and I would have laughed if I wasn't so angry. I just yelled son of a bitch at him and asked him why he didn't tell me. I really didn't need to ask because I knew the answer — he was avoiding upsetting me. Look how well that turned out hey!? Yes, I would have been upset. Not because she was pregnant but because I wasn't and I had just recently had the miscarriage. The moral of this story is if this happens, which is very possible, please let the person you love know what's going on and let her weep, swear and be angry and hold her in your arms tight so she has something to hold on to that is real. That way she can be prepared. My anger didn't last long but it was intense.

Baby or Bust

Razor Resentment now you have a name
I will give you no cause to claim your fame
You have been such a bitter part of my life
The cause and the continuance of much strife

Razor resentment I am now more aware
Of your hatred and how you just don't care
You will do whatever is in your power
To decimate my life any way, hour by hour

Razor resentment I would like to say
That I won't have you back come what may
But that in my heart I don't truly believe
Because I know your skills in how to deceive

Razor resentment you take whatever is good
And make it look like something it never should
You twist the words and thoughts in my mind
So much so that to any goodness I am blind

Razor resentment I so long to say goodbye
But I know you so well that it makes me cry
To leave all that you are and your wickedness
The evil comfort even, sadly I must confess

But it is now time for me to turn my back on you
And walk forward to see with joy what I can do
Without you razor resentment filling up my head
I am free to live in God's will instead.

The Angry Ant

Sure, that's a lot easier said than done, but truly, what choice do you have? Despite the fact that things weren't turning out as planned or hoped for, we needed a new perspective. My punching bag, for a time, was a real asset, but I didn't want to be that bitter person, so jaded and full of cynicism that joy would not be allowed to penetrate. I have met women like that; with the loss of a child and the children they have not living up to their expectations, and they are angry. And scary. The type of person you might be inclined to avoid if you had the choice.

How to avoid becoming a bitter bitch. I had to pray hard about this and ask God to help me forgive. I had to forgive myself because my body was not giving me the gold-standard outcome I so desired. My mind was clouded with one thought, baby or bust. Everything I did, everything I was thinking about, were all directed to that one aim. To have our baby – it was such an overpowering, all-consuming way of life. In a way, it had to be because we wanted success. To get success we had to do things like avoid certain foods, I stopped wearing perfume, I drank fresh vegetable juices more often, and had to get more sleep, and eat healthier. Everything I was doing was overshadowed by that aim. My husband was tired of talking about it, my family were trying to be supportive while giving me the hint that this may not actually happen so please stop hurting yourself in the process.

When we were invited to friends places I didn't want to go a lot of the time. What would I say, "Oh, yeah, I've been working, and yeah, we're still trying to get pregnant. No, not going so good, but you know, it can happen. Or what have you been doing lately? Working, having injections a lot, bit of sex but not enough, ummm what else, honey?" Boring as bats. I just felt boring, bloated and like I was always battling bitterness. Afterward, at home, I would be exhausted and just want to cry.

Some friends we could be very open with about it which made it a lot easier, however it I still avoided going out, and quite often David would go out alone. I was content to stay home with Hawkeye and watch TV or read as it was much easier than having to make an effort to talk or just be around people.

This is something to be aware of, and if you do feel like you're avoiding social situations or being around people, keep a check on it because you run the risk of isolating yourself and potentially losing some strong supports. It's not easy, but friends can provide some light relief and when you're not doing a cycle you can enjoy a drink and let your hair down with them. Believe me you gotta do it.

Time for change.

I was at the Gold Coast visiting my sister Caroline. This was in the latter days of our IVF experience. It wasn't quite over yet, so I was talking to her about it and feeling pretty miserable. We were drinking the most delicious glass of champagne. It was exquisite and felt like silk as it slid down my throat. Nothing but the best for us! My sister was treating me to something special. Anyway we were talking and she stopped and looked at me and said, No, No more". She wiped the tears from my eyes and said No. You have a life, this is not your life. It's not you".

That moment transformed me as I realized that I had been submerged in a place where I was lacking what it took to be me. I guess if the aim was to have a child which it was, then that was my be-all and end-all. I had lost myself in the fog of the pursuit of my quest.

It was a significant shift in my thinking. And this gave me the strength to continue with faith that the outcome whatever it would be, was the right one. It didn't mean I would like it, however, that wasn't the point. I don't think my sister realized the impact she had on me that day. It was like a turning point where I could go down one path – reliant on the outcome of me being a mum or I was nothing, or the other which was to do my best to have a baby but to let the real me shine through regardless. I would still be me – my worth wasn't to be equated with my capacity to have a baby or not.

Chapter 7

Deeds of the Desperate

You may have gathered that my family have always been important to me and have done so much for me over the years. They tried so hard to support me during this time in my life. I talked to my sisters until it became too hard to talk about it and so boring. They thought I was obsessed with the notion of having a baby. My husband thought I was obsessed about having a baby. I *was* obsessed! Okay, I'm not sure I would have admitted it so readily back then, but it was true. But I only had a small window of opportunity and it was closing fast.

I talked to my mum, and she told me my brother's girlfriend was pregnant (thirteen weeks), and she asked how we were going with it all. I changed the subject and moved on. Next topic, please! My brother and sister-in-law never told us or shared with us their struggle with having their baby, and I never asked. I just couldn't handle it, but it never occurred to me that he could've given me the heads up – I didn't expect that from him, whereas from others, I absolutely had that expectation.

Baby or Bust

My family would ask us to come visit and I'd say (to myself) I have to check my cycle and whether I'd be having injections at that time or checkups at the clinic. Bit of a spontaneity dampener, just a tad. I have to say that when we could tee up a time to meet we would celebrate with karaoke, champagne and lots of just being together. We didn't always have the words to say to each other, they didn't know what it felt like to not have a kid of their own, but they loved me and cared. Cared about us both. By the way, Abba is awesome to sing out loud with gusto and enthusiasm, which I did...many times. I'd be singing with my sisters and tears falling, but we just kept on belting those words out, for better or worse. They were just there and that meant a lot.

At my mum's 70th Birthday Party in Melbourne, about two weeks after we had miscarried, I was sitting in the dining room trying to get myself together as we were surrounded by beautiful young healthy nieces and nephews. I really didn't want to be there. My oldest brother walked in the door and looked at me and said, "Hey how are you?" I looked at him, and he hugged me while I cried. We didn't say a word but that hug meant so much to me and gave me strength to be there for my mum.

At this time, I was getting counselling, which is something I highly recommend. If you're doing a cycle, you can possibly see the counsellor at the clinic you attend. I did that briefly, but I discovered that in between cycles, you were not eligible for counselling which to me was so ridiculous. Basically, it meant that the cycle that had not been successful couldn't be discussed until I was doing another cycle which could be a month or two down the track, depending on finances and our capacity emotionally and physically to do it all over again. Check this option but if you can, get a mental health care plan from your GP and engage a psychologist you can see regularly because it helps. You need to be able to say what you can't say to your partner, your family, or even friends. You need an outlet that is safe, confidential, and not easily offended where you can be ugly, snotty, and have the mascara running down your

Deeds of the Desperate

face and not care. Afterwards, you can put on your game face and get on with life.

I cried, swore, spoke candidly and freely about whoever, whatever, and shared my poetry with my counsellor, and she listened, and I felt understood. Having this support enabled me to continue working, although I went part-time for a few months. That was a good strategy as it meant that I could take a day to myself, when my husband was at work, and I could do karaoke (sorry neighbours), cry, walk furiously or lethargically with my dogs, or sit on the lounge and eat and watch TV. No judgement, no pressure and freedom to yell at the TV – better yelling at that then my husband. Freedom to pray earnestly, fervently.

My counsellor asked me to consider a donor egg and suggested I ask my youngest sister whether she would do this for me. The way it happened was surreal. I mean, the expectation was that I could just call her and say, "Hey sis, wanna donate one of your eggs so that I can have a baby? You know how much I want one right!" I can't believe I actually did that. No pressure – much.

The counsellor was pretty adamant that it had to be a younger sister, which made sense, and after all, I had two younger sisters, so surely it was possible. The logic behind this was that the younger the donor, the higher the chance of a more healthier, viable egg. I did ask, and one said she couldn't do it. It must have broken her heart to have to say it. It upset her and me, of course, but I understood. Well, when I returned from bazaking land to my rational mind, I did. She had a husband and two kids of her own, and was working full-time in a very intense job. It wasn't fair of me to ask, but you do things you never expected or even thought about when you're desperate. I spoke to her briefly about this years later, and she said that was an awful decision she had to make. It was a horrible position to be put in, but as I said, desperate times, desperate measures.

Baby or Bust

The second time I tried was with my other younger sister celebrating our nieces 4th birthday. We drank a few (or more) champagnes and we laughed and joked as we decorated the cupcakes for the birthday party happening the next day.

After the excitement had settled we took the kids to the park and my sister Emma and I sat together. It was time for us to work out the details of how she could donate eggs and then carry a baby for me after they were fertilised with my husband's sperm. She had offered a few times over the years and now it was the time as time for me was running out.

The logistics were staggering; I mean, David and I were in Canberra, and she was in Northern NSW. She was a single mum, for crying out loud. But she was keen to help us to have a baby. She had discussed it with our mum and she wanted to do this for me. I wanted her to do this for me. It was the time.

I remember sitting opposite her on that sunny day. I was thinking of all the things she would have to endure to make this happen for me. She would have to have injections, blood tests, hormones pumped into her and trips to Canberra at inconvenient times. She would possibly (I'd say definitely) be off the wall due to the medications and she wouldn't have the luxury of lounging around or taking a day off (which I could do) when she felt it was all too hard. She wouldn't be able to drink alcohol or smoke. She would still have her children to care for, prepare meals, get to pre school, do the washing, cleaning and caring. She did not have another person at home to support her.

I sat in the park on the bench facing her and I stopped. The beautiful ocean was behind her and the sky was a brilliant blue. I remember that feeling so acutely. I thought what am I doing? How can I ask her to do this? Seriously she didn't have a clue what she was taking on. I realised she would have counselling prior to the process, but I knew once it had gone that far she wouldn't back down. She wouldn't want to let me down. I truly could not ask her to give up

Deeds of the Desperate

so much for me. I told her no, I didn't want her to do it. She argued with me and was steadfast and genuine.

We both cried. She cried because she knew how much this meant to me and she wanted to make it happen. I cried because I knew that was my last hope and that it had gone. It was up to me to finish the journey we'd started. I know you'd think I was so desperate for a child that I would have taken this opportunity and run with it and not looked back. It seems bizarre that I just said no when the outcome could have been very different if I had said yes. The truth is, it wasn't the right thing for us to do and I knew it then and now. It broke my heart but I never regretted that decision. I could not put her through it because it would have impacted her two daughters, her ex-husband and her, and if it didn't work I didn't want that burden on her. Thus the journey would be finished but it would be on our own.

My sister-in-law offered to be a surrogate and when we decided not to take that path she offered to donate an egg, but that would be weird as well as illegal (probably), because it would be her egg and her brother's sperm. So weird and so bizarre but welcome to the world of in vitro fertilisation. And I can't believe it but we actually thought about these options and considered them as we problem solved our dilemma. I wasn't thinking straight. It was all about how to get that baby or bust. To me, it sounds whacky now but then it was a potential solution. Check it out, and make a decision. Do it or move on to the next potential solution.

Earlier on as it was becoming evident that maybe a baby was not going to happen to me, my sister, who was about to have her second child, asked me to be a birth partner for her. Hmm, I am sure I was the very least helpful, but I was there and it was a heck of a ride. At the time, I was working as a Youth Worker which included running regular band nights on Friday nights for young people where they could flaunt their talent and shake their heads and dance like in a mosh pit. Can't say that was my scene but hey.

Baby or Bust

I was rostered to work when my sister called at 11 o'clock that morning and said she was having the baby so for me to get there asap. I called my boss and tried to get time off. She said I could go if I could get someone else to fill my place. I called around and one of the guys wasn't answering and he was the more likely one to be available. I had my sister on the phone begging me to get there and unbeknownst to me, she actually called my boss telling her I had to be allowed to go. My poor boss, talk about pressure. I only found this out later.

Anyway I packed as if I was going and planned to travel to Wagga Wagga after my shift at 10pm. Not ideal but it was an opportunity that not everyone gets, and I wanted to be there with her so badly. Anyway, nearer to 6pm I was at work feeling pretty edgy when the other worker finally arrived. My boss gave me the nod and I was out of there. In my car driving at night in the rain, with roadworks. I was exhausted when I arrived, but so happy to be there, and Mum and Emma and I sat up while I had something to eat. We went to bed at 11pm, and at about 2am my sister shook me and said we gotta go now to the hospital. In barely minutes I was dressed, in the car and on the way to pick up the other birth partner, someone who actually had a clue as to what was about to happen.

At the hospital, Emma got into a gown and was pretty much into labour. She had her arm around my shoulder and I seriously thought she might dislocate it with the pressure she was putting on it as the pain hit her. The primeval sounds that emanated from her were noises I had never heard before and never ever since. It was like a guttural crying sound not high pitched but deep and a bit scary. They gave her pain medication and we helped her get into a bath. Now, that was tricky and took some maneuvering, and once we had finally gotten her into the bath she had to get out straight away because the baby was coming sooner than anticipated. So back on the bed and squeezing of my shoulder and weird noises and I was first on the scene privy to the most excruciatingly beautiful moment ever. This little head came peeking through and then her

Deeds of the Desperate

tiny body followed right in front of me. So amazing, so incredible I felt like I was off my head seeing this happening. My sister wanted me to cut the umbilical cord, but I just looked blankly at the nurse when she offered the scissors. I was too stunned and mesmerised to do anything practical. All in all, I'm a very helpful birth partner, that's me. *Not!*

It was a girl and they cleaned her up and put her in a crib. I held the oxygen over her as she was having a little bit of trouble adjusting to life on the outside. I was standing there with this beautiful little creature I had just seen being born. How precious is that? How privileged am I to have had that opportunity and so thankful to my beautiful sister for that. While I was tending to my niece the nurses were chatting with Emma and dealing with the afterbirth (another thing I had no idea about), and I heard her tell them that I was her sister and that I couldn't have kids so she wanted me here as this is probably the closest I would ever get to such an experience. I wanted to tell her she was wrong to say that but instead I pretended I didn't hear. After that, they gave me my little niece and I held her, one of the first people to ever hold her. So blessed I felt and I prayed for her as I held this tiny little bundle. It was an emotional and incredible experience. I am so grateful that she invited me to share that with her.

I wonder

I wonder how long it takes to go from this grief
It doesn't seem to want to leave of its own accord
The alcohol cannot seem to dissipate its strength or hold
It's like having a brick in the bottom of your stomach
And a back pack full of weights holding fast
You try to smile as your feet hit the ground each morning
And think it's another day, I can be happy today, it's ok
Then from the recesses comes this wave of loss, the sting of sorrow
And you still get up, go to work, have coffee, do your job
But you wonder how long will this sadness stay?
You wonder, will it ever go away?

Chapter 8

The Last Hoorah

The Road

Did we miss the turnoff or go the wrong way?
How'd we get here?

It's not the place I wanted to be,
nor the place I dreamt I'd end up

Yet here we are on this road and not
the other we've been trying so hard to reach

I'd ask why but I know there's no point,
for to that question is no ready answer

Instead I look at you and you look at me,
we're still here at the end of this road

Do we sit down, bow our heads and
weep for sadness shame and fear?

Perhaps for a while but not too long,
because my darling – we are still here

Baby or Bust

We planned it for September, you know, get some money together, get our heads and our emotions together. Ooh Yeah! So what we got was an emotionally filled August, periodic and tearful. And lots of fear. As the days drew closer, my emotions ranged from cautious and hopeful, to fearful and despaired. I was scared of so much – scared of being pregnant and scared of how I would react if I didn't get pregnant. I was scared I wouldn't be able to carry successfully, wondering if they would be born with everything intact. *Will I be able to continue working while I'm pregnant? Should I work? How will I manage as a mum? How will I manage as a mum with a disability? Can I do this?*

My counsellor warned me not to get my hopes up. My mum warned me and even asked me why I had to do it. I asked myself that question as I stared at my computer and tried to focus on work and failed. Why do I do this? It's because I have to see this to the end and I can't give up on those two embryos that may become wonderful human beings if given the chance. We had so many eggs harvested (nineteen, which is a lot, I know other women who went through the harvest and got four or five) and while some were not viable and some became unviable after being unfrozen I could not bear the thought of leaving an embryo which was essentially my opportunity to have a child. I couldn't rob or deny them or us that opportunity.

In all of this, I believe God was doing his work in both of us, bringing us closer and able to talk about many difficult topics such as sex, feelings, grief and loss, dreams and hopes for our future. What I wanted with all my heart was to give him a little boy, as we discussed when we were pregnant last year, but who knows what the outcome would be? What I did know was that I had to live in the here and now, laughing with David at his antics and our secret nonverbal language while watching TV together. Being in the spirit of the moment, sharing laughter and hugs in the evenings, cooking meals together and talking and playing with Hawkeye. Relaxing with our friends, doing simple enriching things that are already in my life. Enjoying time with my family and my in-laws and not taking them for granted.

The Last Hoorah

I don't have to be concerned about the IVF treatment. If God wills it, it will work and I shall be pregnant and have one or two children. If God doesn't will it, then it won't work, and it's all over, and I would have done all I could do. I can live with that. I have to trust that God knows the best way for us to fulfil His purpose in our lives. I have no idea how I will react; only God knows, and I pray He will comfort us. Last time when we got the call I hung up looked at David who had guessed anyway from our conversation, and then we both went back to reading and playing PlayStation. I read until I couldn't see because of the tears pouring down my face.

My counsellor had the audacity to be on holiday when I called. I made an appointment for two and a half weeks later and then cancelled it because I couldn't leave work. I had to do my job, sometimes. I spent a lot of time being listless and bored at work, not wanting to be there – not really wanting to be home. Just trying to focus on one thing was so hard when I just wanted to do nothing.

I got my period exactly the date I thought I would. I spent at least a few minutes of each day working out ovulation from Day 1 – 28 August. I don't know why I had to work it out each day – it's like it helped me see if it's getting closer to the day as if knowing would make it more likely to be successful.

I was surprised at how I felt – it was good to have the much-discussed, and I suspected much-debated (in my family) event, finally here. And my mood was almost hyper, chatting with my sister Caroline about the intricacies of the process of IVF, which she declared was fascinating, asking me lots of questions, which I was more than happy to answer. She was genuinely interested in what I was doing and what I was going through.

I phoned the clinic and they told me to come in for a blood test on Day 12, which I did. I was at work and got a call saying I needed to be at the clinic at 7am the next day for an ultrasound and blood test as my estrogen level was looking good for ovulation. They always told me the numbers but they never meant a lot to me, I always waited for their interpretation before I responded.

At the clinic, I was greeted by the receptionist warmly and the nurse called my name. We chatted a bit and I asked her what I shouldn't do to make this have the best chance to work. She didn't answer my question which was no surprise because she wouldn't want to say the wrong thing, I guessed. On the other hand, I thought if you are working in the industry of making babies against all odds, then should you not you be aware of the helpful and unhelpful things to do to maintain a pregnancy.

The next day, it was cold I got up early and left my husband and Hawkeye asleep in bed while I went to the clinic. Upon arrival, the ultrasound unit was still closed up, and the clinic door couldn't be opened because the nurse who was going on holiday tomorrow was already in holiday mode and forgot her keys. I remember her getting a bit stressed but I recall maintaining a cool front.

The Ultrasound clinic opened, and when I went in, the lady said, "You know what to do." I entered the room and got ready. Lying there half covered in a sheet I was so tired I could sleep. I had a bad night last night thinking about work and my dog woke me at midnight because he needed to go to the toilet and at 1:30am I was still trying to enter the world of sleep. I had to pray and use mindfulness techniques to help me.

Anyway, she came in and we noted my endometrium is 15mm thick and there's a very handsome-looking follicle 22 x 26 mm, which is helpful.

I asked her what I should do to help make this work. She says, "Don't do anything strenuous. Just pamper yourself, maybe see a movie. If you walk the dog, do it gently, go out for lunch and be happy." I told her I was taking time off work. She thought that was a good idea because it meant I knew that I had done all I could to make it happen.

The Last Hoorah

I headed to the clinic afterwards and it was hard to find a good vein despite the nurses attempts, strapping my arm, rubbing it, poking my veins with a sharp nail that I told her was hurting me. She tried once and no blood came out. I drank some water and did a quick walk to get the blood pumping. Came back and she still couldn't find a good vein. She called another nurse who succeeded on her second attempt. I was praying for God to make it work because I was over it and didn't want it to interfere with my work day. I left with three little band-aids on my right arm.

That night, my husband came home and I reminded him he has to give me an injection, Pregnyl 5000 – just a shot of hormones that left me wanting to cry. I didn't cry, though. I cooked sausages and bread for tea and watched Doc Martin, who didn't end up getting married. He gave me the injection while he's watching The Simpsons, and pretended to jab me and started laughing. I gave a loud fake laugh to help relieve the tension. He looked at me like I was weird, but he knew what I was doing. He wiped my tummy with an alcohol swab and the smell went straight to my nostrils, making me shudder. I said, "Come on just do it. I'm ready." And he grabbed my stomach and pinches a bit, pushing the needle in. It seemed to take ages to get the stuff into me and I was almost gasping for breath as I realised I had been holding my breath while he was giving me the injection. I cleaned up the mess, we watched TV and I ate dinner while he talked to his sister and nephews on the phone.

I woke up on Saturday with help from Hawkeye who needed to go outside. I go out thinking it had worked out well. I will have time on Wednesday to clean the house before we go to the clinic, and after that I wouldn't be doing any housework. I thought David will be out until 9pm Tuesday night, and when he came home he would have to give me two injections. *Tonight* we started on the Clexane injections so we were really into it now. FYI - Clexane was to help prevent clotting in the developing placenta which can cause miscarriage.

Baby or Bust

The day!

Not much fanfare or fuss. I was asked several times who I was and what was my date of birth. The technician came in and said that only one embryo survived the night so we put in only one — the very last one. It was very matter-of-fact. *Yes, you thought you would have two embryos but now you don't, hence your chance of success has s just halved.* When they said one of the embryos didn't survive, there was barely a blink or acknowledgement; it was okay, one it is, so cop that.

The doctor said my uterus was nice and long and she placed the embryo as far up into it as possible. She said that it looked very good and added, "The last one?"

I said, "Yep. I'm taking time off to chill."

She said, "That's good because if it works that will help and if it doesn't, it'means you can't blame yourself because you did all you could." They said that, but I still blamed myself. But actually, what they say is true, it just takes a while to accept.

I went home, had lunch, then went to bed and slept because I could. And I needed it. I feel exhausted and'so glad I don't have to be a hero anymore. I was thinking, *I am so relieved to be here, the absolute end of the road and the chances are that it won't work.* Not to be a pessimist or even defensive. It's real and I'm being realistic. David came home, got dinner, watched a movie, and I went to bed, then had to get up because I forgot the injection. *Duh!*

I woke up, did pessary, have to lie in bed because the longer I do the more effective they are apparently, and it doesn't leak out. Earlier on, I didn't realise I had to keep pessaries in the fridge, and also they say you should wait for a while, like an hour or at least half an hour after you have put it in before doing anything to let it saturate into your system. I was getting up at 5:30am so I could.

The Last Hoorah

However, when you're working, it's hard to find the time to lie around. I had to get up eventually and have a shower because I felt a bit gritty and had to go get a blood test. I felt anxious, but the lady was nice; I told her a butterfly clip works better, and she had no problem. Big sigh of relief. I got phone call regarding the blood test, progesterone level is 68 which was lovely, she said. To sustain a pregnancy you need 60 plus progesterone level, so I agreed that it was lovely.

Could this be possible? Dare I hope.

Last night I had two injections – the very last Pregnyl injection in my life. I had the usual Clexane too, but that would continue for a bit longer, and if I was pregnant that may be a long while, it could be up to sixteen weeks. I know it sounds odd, especially for me, a needle phobe but I was hoping I would be on these injections for a long time. My tummy looked bruised and mottled. When David asked me where I wanted the injection, I pointed to a spot and said, "In between that mark and that bruise, but not on them as it hurts more."

I wanted to go to church today, but I can't get moving. In fact, I'm going back to bed now. How the heck did I get up at 5:30am do the pessary rest for a bit, make a fresh juice, clean up, have shower, walk the dog, eat breakfast, and go to work. Then come home, make dinner, clean up, do injections, pessaries, fall into bed. Now I am seriously not doing anything.

During this time, we decided I would do absolute rest and my husband would manage the house, so looking back, I discovered a question in my diary.

Q: What is more frustrating than not being able to do things you can see needs to be done?

A: Watching someone else not doing anything about it.

Baby or Bust

Lesson learnt – if you're going to do that, i.e. let someone else do the stuff you automatically do without thinking when it has to be done (according to your timetable), just remember; it ain't gonna happen your way. You're going to have to let it go. It might be the washing not being hung out, the dishes on the sink, or the mess in the lounge room. Whatever it is, you need to somehow not see it because I learnt (the hard way of course) that he will do it and do it well. Just not according to my perfected and practised timelines. It's a conversation to be had – just lie on the lounge, watch TV, eat chocolate (*oh, I mean fruit*), and when he can't find you anymore, he will clear the path.

My family kept in touch regularly and I remember a phone call with Mum, and I was saying how I have been craving avocadoes and her response, "Oh well, it's probably just the season for it."

When I said, "Yeah but I have been craving them a lot."

To which she replied, "Well when you're doing nothing, you tend to eat more." In other words, no acknowledgement that I could be having cravings because I was pregnant. I was annoyed about that, but there was only three more days until I would know for sure. Three days, that's it! We will know if we are going to be a mum and a dad. I keep thinking what a vast difference it will make in our lives – to have a child of our own. To be responsible for another human being who depends on us for everything.

A friend came around and we got the pregnancy books out and read up on where I was up to. It's pretty amazing to think about all that action that is happening; although the level of fatigue I am feeling, I can see where my energy is being invested.

The possibility that this could actually happen increases daily as the progesterone levels increase as pessaries are being properly absorbed into my system. I don't know if you know, but fun fact, pessaries are either inserted into the rectum or the vagina – the

The Last Hoorah

clinical team advises you where it is best for absorption for you - sometimes one, sometimes two.

I believe and trust God to work all this out. I hope David can come out of his seclusion zone and talk to me openly and honestly about his worries and fears. I have noticed my hands have been shaking a bit and my heart rate a bit accelerated, he noticed too which doesn't help matters.

There are possible side effects of Prednisone and Progynova, including breast enlargement, leg cramps, fatigue, and anxiety. Basically, some of the side effects can mimic pregnancy, making me hopeful, too hopeful that I could actually be pregnant. I know this, but still pray that this little one will be a Super Trooper and make it to the final round, i.e. birth, and be with us for many years.

I feel like I am wasting my time here at home, but I know I have to just keep cool and relax, and really I am enjoying not having to rush around, not having to go to work and deal with other people's issues. Not having to run around and do housework and clean up madly. I got annoyed with David because he asked me how I was feeling about— and didn't finish the sentence. — I said, "About what? The baby?" It's like he can't say it, I get it and I think I'm getting annoyed so I can have a change of emotion from fear and sadness. I want to cry but I don't want to cry.

I'm feeling everything in my body, I mean, I'm so conscious of it. Which is probably very natural, but right now, in my lower abs, there's a bit of pain, some sharp stabbing pains but no blood. I feel like my breasts are getting bigger, and I think David noticed when he snuggled into me last night. A nice surprise indeed.

He came home early, got dinner and we ate together in bed. I got the injection stuff ready and he did the Clexane injection for possibly the last time ever. I didn't say that to him as he was already anxious, and when I asked him how he felt, he said, "Stressed." I gave him a big hug and told him it would be okay.

We decided that I would get the phone call and then call him and let him know the outcome. *Maybe I should buy some alcohol while I'm there tomorrow to help dull the pain if necessary*, I think, but I won't do that. I believe if I drink alcohol when I need comfort, I miss out on much better, healthier ways to find comfort. And yeah, that sounds good in theory. If I'm being honest, my strategy would be to have a few drinks and then have sex.

If I am pregnant, it means our life, our marriage will never be the same. It'll be a shock to both of us to have a baby in our home 24/7 and we really have no clue what that means in reality. If it is positive tomorrow and I am pregnant that means the baby will be born in June – wow! Of course there's a lot to go through to get to there. We'll have to take it day by day both of us leaning on God to sustain us.

The day!

The usual start was pessary, resting, and then David dropped me off to get the blood test to determine if we were successful or not. I met my friend afterwards at McDonald's for a bit of breaky, then she dropped me home. I wasn't in a very talkative mood—I just wanted to be alone. I had a cuppa and the proverbial avocado to eat, and watched TV, or at least looked at the TV, my mobile in my lap.

I was watching Jag when the phone rang and I quickly muted the TV. The nurse said, "It came back negative."

I said, "Okay."

She replied, "Well you'll probably be in for an emotional weekend, so I'll call you next week to see how you are."

The Last Hoorah

Just as she said *'it's negative'* David walked in the back door. I looked at him and shook my head. He stood near the lounge and kind of physically braced himself. I finished the conversation and went to him and we hugged. We went back and watched TV.

I asked him how he felt. Sad. I got Hawkeye and put him in the car so we could go somewhere magpie-safe to go for a walk. I tried calling my older sisters but they didn't answer. I sat near the pond and cried. I saw three ladies my age walking with their babies in prams, and I wanted to scream at them "Are you right? Can you f*****g well rub it in any more mate?" Instead, I walked back to the car in a daze.

And so I said to myself as I drove home, "The grieving begins again for the last time." I acknowledged that I'm relieved it's over and I finally know God's answer. Will I have kids Lord? No. Well, why did I have to take all these years and thousands of dollars to get that darn answer? Just a simple *no* would've saved us a lot of heartache and pain. *I have no idea where you're going with all this Lord, what is the point?*

I was thinking, maybe we should go to Cambodia and help kids over there or do something like that but I don't know, I don't know what is next. Anyway, right now I say, "The world is my oyster, and so why not consider these things?" I have my passport ready to leave whenever, wherever. I have time. I'm not going to work next week. The thought of listening to people's sad stories when I am full of sadness is too much to bear right now. I had trouble getting to sleep. I lay staring at our bedroom ceiling, one hand behind my head. Funny how you can just stare and time rolls by. I sent texts to people letting them know the outcome while tears streamed down my cheeks and wet my pillow.

Hawkeye snuggled up with me all night. I got up twice to check on David. He was on the PlayStation; the first time playing a game, the second time he was asleep, but he woke up and came to bed.

Baby or Bust

We lay holding each other close, and then he got on his phone, and I blabbed on saying whatever came out. He listened as he knew that's my way of coping. Eventually, we both slept. Well he did first and then I lay and cried for a while and finally fell asleep with no dreams this time.

A few weeks after, after I had weaned myself off Prednisone, I gathered all the medication including Prednisone, Blackmores Gold, Clexane, Progynova, Pessaries (so glad to say goodbye to them) put it all in a bag and chucked it in the bin. I just had to get it out of my house. After that, I went to bed, cried, slept, woke up, cried, and felt angry. Went to church and cried. Felt angry and did some boxing. Stayed home from work next day. Have a heavy period, which I can only term a bitter irony in the face of my desire to become a mother being so finally and absolutely thwarted.

Chapter 9

Return to Life

It's Time

There comes a time as Neil Young said
Where you have to put the issue at hand to bed
Those were not exactly Neil's words or intentions
It's just a phrase of which I made mention
Regardless the fact remains that It's all over now, baby blue
And for us having our own child is over too
The battle has been fought with long stand offs for over 10 years
Words raised in anger, pillows punched and many, many tears
I wonder what will be left when the dust settles
A relationship of warmth or armour lined with metal
I have a dream, in the words of Martin Luther king
Our dream's been beaten up, pulverised and boy does it sting

Baby or Bust

It is now thirteen years since we finished our IVF journey and so much has happened in that time. I have been working with people with mental health issues and learning a lot. I finally finished my Social Work degree in 2015, and celebrated this at my graduation. It was an amazing day as it reminded me that I could achieve many other dreams and I was doing it. I have travelled to lots of places, fallen in love with Paris and am keen to return and see more of this incredible world we live in.

In the next few pages, I have shared excerpts from my journey of recovery, which was neither straightforward or easy. I haven't put it in chronological order purposely because in reality I was all over the shop feeling great one second and the other not, but as my mum would say, "Nothing worthwhile is ever easy." I have tried doing different things only to find I wasn't ready and had to retreat a bit to heal some more before venturing into unknown territory again but persistence pays off. I am looking forward to many more adventures, after all, it's my life!

What not to do on your return to life after IVF.

So about three years after we finished, I went to a training day about pregnancy loss and IVF thinking I could use this for my social work or even in the church I attended. I mean, who knows maybe I can use this experience and help others. That was my rationale for being there, however it was so hard to sit there and listen to a woman talking about my experience from an outside perspective. I really wanted to be up there telling people how it was and will be afterwards when you're left chiildless, and it's not discussed anymore. It's all so tiring and so painful. It's like the grief has come flooding back with a vengeful spite just to make sure I don't forget about how bad it was.

I sat there listening to this talk on ethics and 'when does a child become a child?' And I know in my heart that when those embryos were implanted they were potential human beings, otherwise why the hell do you go through it?

Return to Life

So what was I feeling sitting there apart from *I really need to get the heck out of here before I really lose the plot*. I was trying to look at it from an objective perspective, that was my aim anyway. In reality, all objectivity was washed away by the tears flowing and my struggle to breathe. It had been three-and-a-half years, and there I was. I thought I could handle doing this but I was so not ready.

I called David but he took forever to get there to pick me up. I was upset because I needed him and he knew where I was, so I figured he should have been more attentive. Anyway, instead while I was waiting I called my sister, who proceeded to ask me if I heard the news about my niece, which made me want to scream. I really didn't need to hear someone else's good news when it would never happen to me, and really did you have to tell me right now? She was instantly sorry she'd said it when I said, "Yeah, she's pregnant that's great," in a flat, almost angry tone. *What is going on with me? I am so off the planet I can't seem to get it together.* It was a cause for celebration; my beautiful niece was pregnant and my sister was excited about it. All very normal — but at that moment I couldn't handle it.

Where do we go from here?

The end is the hardest part. Realising you will never ever have kids is the hardest time. It's the time when you want to change everything so that your life is different from what you dreamt, but it was you who made it different. It wasn't just that you couldn't have kids that made your life different. In your search for some control over this, so-out-of-your-hands situation, you seek to gain some control. Some people leave their spouses and pursue others in the hope that life will be better. The rose-coloured glasses are ripped off, and the romantic comedies don't appeal to you because they're not anywhere near reality. I ended up watching shows and reading books that were hard biting, cynical and that justified my own growing cynicism and say that's the way it is. Lots of death, my dog dying, my bird dying, my pet mice dying, my babies dying. All my brothers and sisters have kids. What have I got left? Who am I?

I spoke to the lady from Barnardos, and we determined that as we have been doing fertility treatment, we won't pursue foster care for twelve months, which is a very big relief to me. Now, I don't even have to think about whether fostering is something I want to do again at all. I told my counsellor that even when I have sex I want to use condoms to prevent even a remote hope of getting pregnant. I don't want to hope anymore.

One month later…

So now it's one month later and I'm still here. The nightmare has happened, but I'm still alive, I'm going to work and doing my job. In between reading mediocre books and watching television until I fall asleep, hardly speaking to my husband or my dog, and praying has gone right out of the window. I get up, get ready for work, pretend to work, come home, cook dinner, tidy up or not. Watch TV, read, write, go to bed. The next day, the same thing happened with minor variations. I don't sound too excited about life at all, probably because I'm really, really not.

Today I'm home from work and really don't care I have fought tears and sobs all week that needed to be let out so I can get on with my life and adjust to this change in me, my perceptions and my dreams for the future. The old dream is gone. Now, I need to adjust to the new dream, the only thing is I don't know what I hope for. What do I aspire for now? My life is not over but that chapter is, and it being over is not all bad. At least now we know exactly where we stand. We're not having our own kids we don't know why, yet there it is.

> ### *Where to?*
>
> *Where to from here? I'm forty-three and want to know. I want to know the meaning of life and it ain't forty-two because I've been there and found nothing but sadness. Like a blanket that covers or rather one that smothers. Like walking through honey with a pair of flippers, not getting very far and too much effort to sustain. Sitting in my pyjamas all day watching TV, eating and drinking lots of tea. Am I just pining, feeling sorry for myself, wallowing in the sadness and the grief? When do I wake myself up from this foggy greyness and see that the sun is shining, the sky is blue and there's so much life to be had?? I say now, and not later in some fictitious time frame that never abounds.*

The Tumultuous Tapestry of a New Beginning

> ### *The Smile*
>
> *We talk, we laugh and walk hand in hand. Our conversation flows about nothing and everything enjoying the touch of your hand enclosing mine as we walk with the dog. He's straining to stop and sniff but we maintain a brisk pace and the air is cool on our faces. I feel the first beads of sweat forming marking the beginning of warmer days to come.*

We finished our last cycle in September 2011, and in January 2012 we went on our first overseas trip. It was a cruise to New Zealand and we went with my mother and father-in-law. Having that to look forward to went a long way to helping us begin to begin to recover. Grief affects everyone differently, and when you're grieving you do it at your pace, your way.

Baby or Bust

Your partner may not even appear to be sad or grieving at all. Watching my husband it took me a while before I realised that he was grieving in his own way. I had to give him space to not talk about it. I'd want to talk to him so badly but he wasn't ready. I had to talk to others in order for me to get what I needed to help me deal with my grief.

It was a hard lesson to learn, to just leave it and he would talk when he was good and ready. It was never soon enough for me, but it is not something you can force, and if you try, it can lead to heated arguments and hurtful things being said, so it really is not worth it. I encouraged him to see a counsellor and I'd like to say I left it at that, but hey, you can benefit from my experience.

The cruise was exciting, and my mum-in-law and I danced and sang karaoke with such exuberant enthusiasm we got a rousing applause. Maybe it was because we'd finished and were exiting the stage. Hmm! It was so much fun. The husbands were on the sidelines cheering us on, hoping we would get it out of our system quickly but we went back for more. I loved being on the ocean and the fresh air, the sunshine and the amazing beauty of New Zealand. It was like a new beginning where we could take time to recalibrate and start to heal.

When we returned home, we enrolled in an art class. Neither of us had any idea how to draw or paint but doing this inspired us to do more. My first still life amazed me because I hadn't used charcoal before, I had no clue. It made me reevaluate what I might be capable of and the absolute joy of being in the zone was addictive. People who say they can't draw really might be surprised. With the right help, I reckon they could. The best thing was that we were going to classes together and it was a good talking point far away from cycles, injections, babies and all the sadness.

Joyful! Just me, a canvas and some charcoal. At times I would forget about everything and just enjoy the learning, the subject and the objective — to create something from nothing. I could do that! Sometimes, I would draw and cry with my back to the others, and that was okay too. That was the incredible thing. The blank canvas and me – and I was creating things, drawing pictures of naked women, and even a naked man on one occasion, *shock horror or oo lala*!

I would have a frisson (I have always wanted to use that word somewhere) of fear and excitement as I would begin. I never knew what was going to happen on the canvas, it was so thrilling to see that piece of fruit on the table in front of me now on my canvas. Drawn by me and even more thrilling, it actually looked like a piece of fruit. WOW!

In June 2012 our precious little Hawkeye died. His death brought back a crushing sense of loss and an emptiness to our home. I knew he can never be replaced – and wondered if I could love another dog again? I say you can't not have pets because there's a risk of losing them, like with people. Instead, what do you do? You live, you love them with all your heart and you count yourself so blessed by having them in your life for so long, however long. My baby was seven weeks, and I treasured every moment, every feeling, every change in my body and never, not for an instant, have I regretted being blessed with pregnancy despite the despair of the loss. So many losses, yet God is still on the throne and directing my life in spite of me.

At work, I facilitated a support group for women with mental health issues, Women Supporting Women, and it included collaging and being creative. I have included a photo of one of my collaging attempts. I found it enjoyable as it helped me to express how I felt without me having to think too much. This was way before I did an art classes so I was more keen than skilled at this, however, it was cathartic.

Baby or Bust

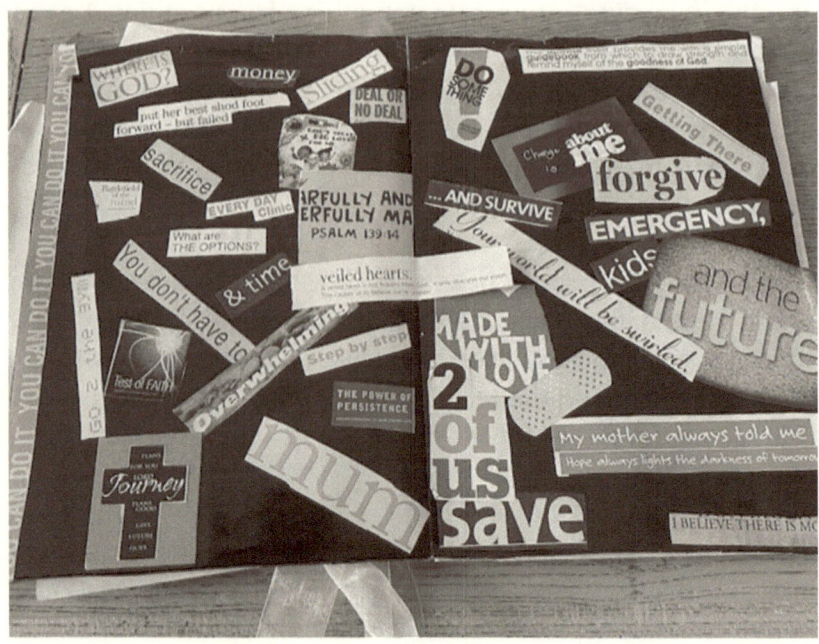

Collaging my experience of grief helped me to be able to maintain my job during the years we took doing IVF. I wrote in my diary and wrote poetry as a means of getting the sorrow out of me and to give me room for hope. I couldn't share what was happening to me with the group, however I did tell them about the miscarriage. One of the ladies said to me, "Maybe you're not meant to have kids because we need you here. If you had a kid, you would be focused on that, which would leave us without your support.. Maybe that's what you're meant to be doing." That was pretty profound, I reckon because I have worked with a lot of people over the years, and it has been amazing. Food for thought.

Meanwhile back at the ranch...David was playing on the computer and watching TV while I cried and stomped around like an angry bear on the loose. At times, I felt very distant from him, but other times I felt this experience was bringing us closer together. Him, getting me dinner and looking after me while we waited to find out if I was pregnant made me feel loved and cared for. Now, I was

Return to Life

afraid he would go on like nothing had changed, when in my mind, everything had changed. Everything and nothing.

After Hawkeye died, that left us with no caring responsibilities and when my mum ever so casually hinted that she'd love to go to Italy and perhaps Paris with someone, well, we were keen. I organised that trip, and I tell you it was the best thing and took me out of myself, away from the constant grief and into the beginning of a new future filled with exciting new adventures. Not the ones we had planned exactly, but hey, a trip to Europe is an awesome opportunity. Here are some photos of us having fun. I tell you, fun is so great. I loved that we got to travel to amazing places with my mum, and there's so much more I could say, but that's another story.

So maybe you're thinking that after five years I should be able to manage and go to work and be able to move on. Our very good friends have invited us to their baby's first birthday in February, and I haven't given them an answer yet. I want to go because they are our friends and he is such a gorgeous little boy. But I don't know if I can

face it with their happiness rubbing in my face. One of the women who will be there has two children via IVF, and another with two children is a woman who I prayed for as she was having a hard time getting pregnant. It's just not fair but that's just the way it is. I don't have to go, and I'm sure she will be okay with that, but my dilemma is: Do I let this stop me this time and again next time, or do I bite the bullet go to the party, be all happy and then come home and be a wreck? I dunno if I want to bother. Does it get easier each time I do these things?

Another day...

I have watched about seven hours of TV today and am still watching. I think I'm feeling depressed and I really don't enjoy being like this. What makes me smile right now? I can't think of anything offhand. I feel isolated from David in more ways than I care to say.

I got diagnosed with situational depression during this time. Fortunately, I was able to manage it with counselling and putting structure into my day so I didn't have to think too much. Just do what had to be done. I remember going for a walk and actually seeing, as if for the first time, that the sky was blue. It was as if a haze of grey had filtered my view for so long and then suddenly I saw it for real. The absolute vast beauty of the blue sky, it was an amazing revelation and part of the start of my return to life.

Return to Life

I'd like to say I prayed a lot for healing. I think I did but praying was a bit spasmodic for a while. I never doubted that God knew what he was doing and that he was in control and that all things would work out for the best according to his plan, not mine. I know my mum was angry with God for a long time about it but I told her not to go there. There's always a reason these things happen or don't happen.

During this time a new client asked me if I had any kids. Of course, it's just a question that people ask, no big deal. Much! I felt like running out the door telling her to rack off and to mind her own business. Just so you know, I actually sat, deliberately stayed in my seat and said, "That remains to be seen." And that was the end of that conversation. I'm not good at hiding my feelings at the best of times and that day was not the best of times.

Grief

Have you met grief he asked as I stumbled brokenly to the door. Oh no I think I remember meeting grief before. Ah, is he related to loss? I really wanted to know. Hmm he nodded sagely Where grief is, loss tends to go. If it's not too rude I'd like to ask grief to go to hell. I've had it with his stronghold and keeping me unwell. Please tell me is there any chance to avoid meeting him I say. He turned and looked at me and said No there really is no way. But what do I do when this grief and loss keep pummelling me, I tried to run I tried to hide but everywhere they see.

You have to stop he cried with passion in his voice. You have to stop and face them. There really is no choice. Look at them squarely- both grief and loss in the eye. Stand tall, be bold, have courage, don't be shy. It's time to meet them, both grief and loss and to shake their hand. Only by doing this will they lose their power of command.

Baby or Bust

> ### *No Sarcasm Here*
>
> *There it is motivation. Oh no it's gone*
> *Here comes apathy, grab a cuppa, and lie on the couch until sadness drops tears and then weeping and sobbing join in. A crescendo that quakes your entire body bringing muscle tension visiting with vengeance after which exhaustion settles in and hangs around constantly. And when you try to sleep him off, insomnia with his brass band and reel to reel thoughts arises uninvited, unwanted and unceasing. Until anger crashes in splatting and shattering, swearing profuse profanities, lashing out loudly recklessly at whatever or whoever is still around after all this time.*

Maybe this is yet another stage of grief where you have longer periods of time when you feel normal, good even, and then you fall in a heap and can't seem to crawl your way to the door. You feel like, "Oh no haven't we been there done that." I have been keeping my mind busy with reading lots of books, and working, and cooking dinner, and cleaning up. I'm watching TV and going out as well, maybe too busy trying not to feel the emotions until I'm left shaking, unable to think clearly or focus, and with tears falling from my eyes and no way to control it.

I believe our kids are in heaven and it was (is) God's will that we wouldn't have our own children here on Earth. And it does get easier. I miss my Hooli and Hawkeye in these times because we had them to hold. Now we have little Jazz, (he's a dog, yes, I am aware of that. He's not a baby; he's a dog). He's my little boy whom I can love because he's here, and he needs me, and I need him. He snuggles into me, and his head relaxes on my shoulder, and he sighs a happy sigh. That's probably the closest I'll get to a baby so I take it gladly. I've come to the end – No baby, no Hawkeye, just me, David, and Jazz. A new era, a new beginning, a new year, new hope, new Church.

Return to Life

One year today since we finished IVF, ended our dreams and hopes of ever having our own child. Spent today reading novels in bed and eating ice cream. We had roast chicken for dinner, didn't talk much. Not much to say, really, except that not having Hawkeye here with me anymore makes these times even harder. He died six months after we finished treatment. It set me back into grief again. It's like you feel like you're just getting a grip on life and getting back on track and then BAM. He died and the acuteness of losing him brought back the grief of all our babies and the other members of our menagerie, and you feel like you're in a Batman and Robin cartoon– whack, zap, bam, kaboom.

Sometimes I feel like I'm drowning or submerged in a fog or dark pit. I'm trying so hard to climb out and to see the light, and just when I think I have got a foothold, I fall down, again. I think, *why cry anymore? It doesn't change the fact that we can't have kids or that our beautiful dogs are dead.* It's so hard to contain my tears — I guess if I don't cry I feel like I'll just break up in pieces. And so I cry...I wonder if tears ever run out of salt.

Getting back

I'm making my way back to the land of the living
There's so much for me to do, stop taking and start giving
Doing one small kind act for someone each day
No matter if it's acknowledged I'm not doing it for the pay
Part of my healing, part of getting me out of myself
Not hiding in my little house, gathering dust on the shelf
Sometimes I feel I'm not enough, I'm running out of me
Don't have what it takes, maybe that's it,
Lord where you want me to be

Baby or Bust

Since it happened, I have come a long way. I'm now going out, I'm doing Nutrimetics and meeting people. But I gotta tell you, there are moments where the pain catches me and takes my breath away, and I realise I've got a long way to go. I'm sure it will get easier and I know how far I've come. It has been a struggle to keep it together at work but I have been doing well and more focussed, which is an improvement. Now I have to keep my mind focussed on the good things I have going on in my life i.e. Paris and Italy (Yay!), which is happening less than a week tomorrow. There is life without being a mum - I haven't got to the place of acceptance quite yet, but I am moving in that direction and with God's help I can keep going. I purchased a charm for my Pandora – it's a gift box tied with a ribbon and symbolises all of our babies. Gifts from God that we can't see now. In the future we will see our children. I feel happy about that.

Some days I'd be thinking, *hey I am doing okay. I'm at work talking, doing my thing and then.* Slap, bang. I ran into an acquaintance who asked me if I was pregnant. Just like that. My response was to burst into tears, and unfortunately for her, I genuinely couldn't stop. I was trying to say, "No, I'm not, sorry I am crying," but I just had to walk away. I really lost it, I just wept. I also felt like a fat blob because I was damn well not pregnant. *Seriously, timing people.* Of course, she didn't know, she was thinking how wonderful it was because she really thought I was pregnant and she would have been happy for me.

> *No use surmising of the way things might have been. What is, is and if that's the case and it's all over I look forward to waking up with a heart full of joy not sadness where I get out of bed and all seems OK but in myself I know as I eat my breakfast cereal that I'm not. I'm not the same person I was before. Before when? you could well ask. I guess the answer would be before the end and the realisation that is not meant to be. I still say it's OK to dream and pray and you can hope. It's not for naught, despite the heaviness of empty arms.*

Return to Life

As I'm writing this, it's been thirteen years since we finished IVF. I'm sure things have improved with technology since we were there and I know of women who are going through it right now and pray for their success. As for me, I have so longed to share my story and now it is done.

If I die soon what would I regret? Would I regret wasting so many tears and time worrying about my marriage or lack of children? I think I would like to leave the world with an impact that God can give you hope even in the depths of despair and darkness .If I look at life as being part of eternal, then having children or not is of no consequence, having a perfect marriage or not doesn't matter either. It's what I do with what I have that matters.

Afterword

(the final word or conclusion)

Thank you for reading my book. I hope that you found it helpful and to expand on that I am including some discussion questions to help you consider how you are right now. Maybe you are starting or in the thick of IVF or at the end of the journey. Maybe you have a baby or perhaps this didn't happen for you or your sister/friend etc. The questions are for you and your family members, friends etc for them to consider from their perspective. Grief is not a one size fits all process, nor is it a straight path. While I have shared a few thoughts in relation to each question everyone will have something different to say.

How do you react when things are not going the way planned? What are you feeling in that moment? How would others know what you're feeling? Do your family or friends talk to you about your behaviour?

Let me start with the last bit. My husband felt like he was being used purely as a baby-making machine; my family said I was obsessed with having a baby, and they were worried for my physical and mental health. My boss and colleagues at work, who were aware of what I was doing, were supportive and compassionate, but I still had to do the job. That was fair enough; it wasn't easy to focus on others at times, but the structure of going to work was helpful as it was predictable and there, at least, I felt like I had some control and autonomy. My friends at Church prayed with me and for me, and we were able to talk about it with a few close friends, but that got boring and tiring after a while, for everyone. I mean, we did it for five years, so the topic was old, so I just stopped talking about it to anyone other than my family.

In my book, I note some of my reactions to things not going well, i.e. anger, frustration, and the build-up of resentment towards my husband and God. My family, particularly my sisters were often at the other end of the phone listening to me cry. I hated upsetting them as they didn't want to see me hurting. My mum got angry with God. My dad and my brothers knew what was going on although we didn't talk much but I knew they only wanted the best for me.

> *For I know the plans I have for you, declares the Lord, plans to prosper you and not to harm you, plans to give you a hope and a future. Jeremiah 29:11*

Have your relationships changed with your spouse/partner/family members/friends/God etc? In what way have they changed and how does this impact on you now?

I think what helped us was intentionally doing fun things together with my husband like attending an art class and doing an Italian cooking course. I'd like to say we prayed together regularly, but we didn't. However, we both prayed and that, I believe it has sustained us. I used Stormie O Martian's "The Power of a Praying Wife" to help direct my prayers away from my anguish and to focus on the goodness that God was doing amidst the turbulence.

My family were all relieved that it was over and we could get on with our lives because when you're in it, you feel like you're in a

Afterword

holding pattern, waiting for something to happen and to some extent, others feel like they are waiting with you.

> *Do not use harmful words, but only helpful words, the kind that build up and provide what is needed, so that what you say will do good to those who hear you.*
> *Ephesians 4:29*

How supported did you feel during the process? What was helpful for you? Do those who supported you know that their help made a difference?

A lot of the time I felt alone going through it despite the support I had. I didn't seek support from services as I was avoiding people as much as possible and felt it was too hard for me to face others at the time, plus I couldn't find any that I wanted to check out enough to summon the energy to try. Maybe it would have been different if I had, however this is over fifteen years ago and now I believe there are more supports available and from what I have seen, they look relevant and have lots of resources.

Recently, I linked with Bears of Hope, and ordered their package to help us to remember our little ones. The bear is on display discreetly in my home and I find comfort in that. Their care package helped me feel connected to others who had been through a similar experience.

My counsellor was wonderful. She had done IVF, so she knew what was what, and boy, did that help me. I cannot emphasise enough about the importance of having someone to talk to throughout this process.

Does any aspect in the poem Razor Resentment resonate with you/your experience?

Baby or Bust

Writing that poem was a cathartic experience for me because it helped me recognize the bitterness I was at risk of succumbing to and being suffocated by it, so much that I wouldn't be me anymore. I like me and I didn't want that to happen nor would I wish that on anyone else.

> *Watch out that no poisonous root of bitterness grows up to trouble you, corrupting many. Hebrews 12:15*

How do you express grief? What helps/hinders you in expressing how you feel when you are grieving?

Some cultures express grief loudly and publicly and it is accepted. I like their style. I wasn't able to publicly acknowledge the loss of my unborn baby. Instead, I did my own ceremony at the pond, which helped. I wrote about it and I talked to some of my friends and family. My husband and I supported each other as much as we could but it was a struggle to keep going to work and continue being us, a couple with no kids and feel oay about it. I was glad I could talk to God about it.

How to express grief safely – have somewhere you can yell, cry, punch pillows, or a punching bag, go to the gym, cycle, sing sad songs, sing happy songs, laugh, watch sad movies that make you cry so you can release those painful tears. Go outside and watch the sunset, look at the moon and stars, go for a run, swim, dance, walk. Be alone at times, but don't isolate yourself from those who are unsure what to do, what to say. Let them hug you and make you another cup of tea even if you're tea'd out.

> *The Lord is near to the broken hearted and saves the crushed in spirit. Psalm 34:18*

Afterword

Have you seen anything good coming out from your experience?

In a few of my poems I stated that I was different now than before we started. I learnt a lot about myself and marriage and how I handle(or don't handle) stress. For better, for worse type stuff. I felt the stifling barrier of depression, and that experience helped me work more effectively with people. Once I could see through the fog, I had a flicker of hope, and that grew as the fog lifted and the depression eased. My relationship with my husband is stronger, and my faith is stronger.

For those who have had a child through IVF, I wonder if there are unvoiced feelings of grief and loss for the other cycles that didn't go according to plan? On one hand it's expected that you would be happy but there may be unexpressed sorrow.

I have a friend who has three children but had a miscarriage in between. Each year she commemorates her baby's anniversary. While she celebrates the wins, acknowledging the loss and not dismissing it is helping her healing.

One lady told me she had a friend who got pregnant via IVF at the same time she fell pregnant naturally. They were excited because they were going to share the experience of pregnancy. When it didn't work out for her friend she felt guilty because she was still pregnant and her friend wasn't. She didn't know how to handle it and this resulted in them not talking for a long time.

> *God is our refuge and strength, a very present help in touble. Psalm 46:1*

Resources and Support Networks

Get Support where you can. Different services for different people. See the list below. I have also included some books that I found helpful.

Next Step – a Cognitive Behaviour Therapy (CBT) based counselling that is short term and free

The Pink Elephant Support Network – pinkelephants.org.au

Red Nose Grief and Loss Support. Fathers of loss 24/7 support and resources for families/partners

Bears of Hope – grief workshops/dad support

Books

The Power of a Praying Wife – Stormie O Martian

After Miscarriage – Medical Facts and Emotional Support for Pregnancy Loss – Krissi Danielson Harvard Common Press 2008

Baby or Bust

Good Grief – A Constructive approach to the problem of loss Desbooks Publisher Revised edition 1992 – Granger E Westberg

Coping with Grief – The trusted classic guide for the bereaved and their loved ones 4th Edition – Mal McKissock and Dianne McKissock, ABC Books 2012

Grieving the Child I never Knew – a devotional companion for comfort in the loss of your unborn or newly born child – Kathe Wunnerberg. Publisher Zondervan 2001

About the Author

Louise Kearins is a Christian and a woman with a disability and a staunch advocate for people with disabilities. Trained as a Social Worker, she has worked with people from a wide range of backgrounds, including people with disabilities, people with mental health issues, older persons, families and youth, and with National Disability Insurance Scheme (NDIS) participants. She has worked in both Government departments and in the Community sector, including managerial roles, sharing her passion for recovery and hope, encouraging her team to build capacity when working with people and supporting them to achieve their goals in life.

In her spare time she enjoys spending time with her dogs, swimming, reading books and attends two book clubs monthly. She also loves going for motorbike rides with her husband, karaoke and drinking good coffee with friends.

She writes her story of the struggle to have a child and the lengths she went through to achieve this including IVF, to only end up empty handed. It is a story that tells it like it is without blame and gives hope to those with fertility issues that life is doable and can be fulfilling even without your dream of having a child being realised. It is a useful read for family and friends as it gives insight into the experience that can help you understand how it is from the perspective of the person you are trying to care for and support.

https://babyorbustjourney.com/

LOUISE KEARINS

Louise is a dedicated Social Worker, author, and tireless advocate and mental health practitioner who works with people experiencing severe mental health challenges, including those who have had a suicide attempt. With extensive experience in the field, Louise combines compassion, understanding, and practical guidance to empower people during the most difficult times of their lives.

Louise draws deeply from her life experience to inform her work and writing. Her journey through IVF, which did not result in the family she and her husband David had hoped for, inspired her to write her debut book, Baby or Bust. In this candid and heartfelt memoir, she offers a voice to those facing similar struggles, providing solace, hope, and the reassurance that they are not alone.

Louise's advocacy extends beyond her professional and literary pursuits. Living with a disability, she brings a unique perspective of lived experience to her interactions, fostering deep connections with others through empathy and shared understanding. At home Louise finds joy in spending time with her very active schnauzer puppies, motorbike rides with her husband and loves spending time on the beach.

Through her dedication to creating positive change, Louise inspires hope and elicit resilience, one conversation, one person at a time. Her work is a testament to her belief in the power of the human spirit and faith to overcome life's challenges.

TOPICS

1. Mental Health and Resilience: Louise could share her experiences working with individuals who have faced severe mental health challenges, including those who have attempted suicide. She could discuss strategies for building resilience, the importance of compassion and empathy, and ways to empower individuals to overcome their struggles.

2. The Journey of IVF and Infertility: Louise could share her personal story of going through IVF and the emotional struggles that came with it. She could discuss the importance of support systems, the impact of infertility on relationships, and ways to cope with the emotional ups and downs of IVF.

3. Disability Advocacy and Empathy: Louise could discuss her experiences living with a disability and how they have shaped her perspective on life. She could also discuss the importance of empathy and understanding in building connections with others and share ways that she has advocated for disability awareness and inclusion in her personal and professional life.

These topics would allow Louise to share her expertise, personal experiences, and passion for creating positive change, which would make for engaging and thought-provoking discussions.

🌐 www.babyorbustjourney.com ✉ babyorbustjourney@gmail.com

Notes

Baby or Bust

Notes

www.ingramcontent.com/pod-product-compliance
Lightning Source LLC
Chambersburg PA
CBHW030330080526
44584CB00012B/800